G000136655

Cambridge Marketing Handbook:
Communications

Cambridge Marketing Handbook: Communications

Steve Bax & Paul Woodhouse

Publisher's note

Every possible effort has been made to ensure that the information contained in this book is accurate at the time of going to press, and the publishers and authors cannot accept responsibility for any errors or omissions, however caused. No responsibility for loss or damage occasioned to any person acting, or refraining from action, as a result of the material in this publication can be accepted by the editor, the publisher or any of the authors.

First published in Great Britain and the United States in 2013 by Kogan Page Limited in association with Cambridge Marketing Press.

120 Pentonville Road London N1 9JN United Kingdom	1518 Walnut Street, Suite 1100 Philadelphia PA 19102 USA	4737/23 Ansari Road Daryaganj New Delhi 110002 India

www.koganpage.com

© 2013, Cambridge Marketing College.

The right of Cambridge Marketing College to be identified as the author of this work has been asserted by them in accordance with the Copyright, Designs and Patents Act 1988. Edited and proofread by Charles Nixon, Melissa Nixon and Emma Garland. Diagrams redrawn by Kirsty Jones and Jenna Squire.

ISBN   978 0 7494 7061 6
British Library Cataloguing-in-Publication Data

A CIP record for this book is available from the British Library.
Design and layout by Cambridge Marketing College
Printed and bound by CPI/Antony Rowe, Chippenham Wiltshire.

About the authors

Steve Bax DMS MCIM AMRS FCMC Chartered Marketer

Steve is the Managing Director of Bax Interaction, a marketing research, strategy and training company based in Cambridge. He has over 30 years' experience at senior and board levels in B2B, B2C and not-for-profit organisations. Steve has been a tutor for Cambridge Marketing College since 1993, a leading centre for the delivery of Chartered Institute of Marketing courses. He teaches to post-graduate level and currently delivers modules including marketing information and research, project management in marketing, managing marketing and marketing leadership and planning. He has previously also delivered the Market Research Society advanced certificate.

Steve is a long standing member of the CIM, a Chartered Marketer, an associate member of the Market Research Society and a Fellow of the Marketing College. Previously, he has worked as a CEO/CMO for a leading food exhibition company, Head of Marketing for a £25m retail and manufacturing business, Head of a Research and Planning department and Manager of three business units for a £200m home improvements business.

Paul Woodhouse BA (Hons) ACIM ACIPR

Paul is the Group Marketing Manager for the Vindis Group, a family owned motor group with a network of 17 dealerships across East Anglia. These include Bentley, Audi, Skoda, Volkswagen and Volkswagen Commercial Vehicle centres. He joined the company in May 2012 and managed a team of five Marketing Co-ordinators. He is responsible for the centralised marketing of the Group, including the strategic planning and implementation of its marketing programmes.

With a background in journalism and PR, Paul moved into marketing and has worked for a number of agencies and organisations in B2B, B2C and not-for-profit sectors. Despite having all-round knowledge and experience within the full promotional mix from digital marketing to offline, Paul still has a passion for writing and regularly contributes to the Cambridge Marketing Review including profile pieces, interviews and articles, as well as, writing articles, white papers and other thought leadership pieces for Cambridge Marketing College.

Paul is an alumnus of Cambridge Marketing College having completed the CIM Professional Diploma in Marketing in 2012 and is a member of both the Chartered Institute of Marketing (CIM) and the Chartered Institute of Public Relations (CIPR) having completed qualifications in both disciplines.

Paul can be followed on Twitter @pgawoodhouse, on LinkedIn and contacted via email pgawoodhouse@hotmail.com.

Contents

Word clouds produced through Wordle™ (www.wordle.net)

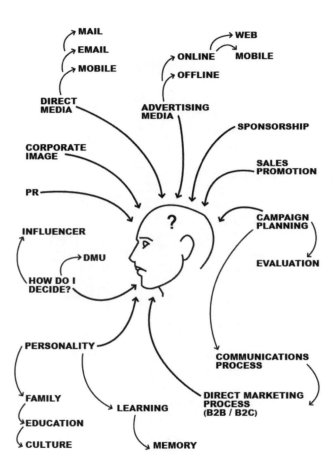

Infographic drawn by Lorna Brocklesby

Acknowledgements

With especial thanks to Cambridge Marketing College tutors – Terry Nicklin, Paul Cowell, Robert Lowther and Edward Ryder for the use of their slides and content in this Handbook.

Introduction

This Handbook is about Marketing Communications. It introduces the key concepts and tools available to marketers to communicate with their marketplace, and looks at the tactics and strategies involved in planning, implementing and evaluating a marketing communications campaign and brand strategies.

It is divided into two parts the first focusing on marketing communications and the second on buyer behaviour. All organisations need to communicate with the wide range of stakeholders who have an interest in their activities; whether these are customers, potential customers, shareholders or employees. But how do you decide what your message should be, which media to use to reach your audience and even who your audience is? And, of course, communication should not just be one-way!

The second part focuses on buyer behaviour – essential knowledge for any marketer and key to deciding how to communicate with your marketplace. How can you affect customer behaviour without understanding their motivations, influences and decision making processes? What models can you use to understand the communications process and how people learn and respond?

Of course, marketing communications is a huge subject – indeed to some, marketing communications *is* marketing! In reality marketing communications is just one element of the Marketing Mix – Promotion – and needs to be managed in line with all the other Ps: Product, Price, Place, People, Process and Physical Evidence. It has not been possible to examine every aspect of this huge subject in this single Handbook but if the topics whet your appetite for more information you will find a wide range of references to follow up and help you communicate more effectively with all of your stakeholders.

Part 1: Marketing Communications

Chapter 1: The Purpose of Marketing Communications

Marketing communications have a wide range of purposes from raising awareness and providing information, to encouraging and persuading customers to buy, to building brands and communicating with internal stakeholders. This chapter looks as some of the key purposes.

1.1 To engage customers and stakeholders

A primary role of marketing communications is to engage audiences. In the first instance, one-way communication enables target audiences to understand the core message an organisation is trying to establish about its brand, product or service. This is achieved through providing information that is of interest or concern, guiding and supporting stakeholders through changes in the organisation's plans and communicating support for their causes and agendas.

The market or target audience may be:

- a consumer audience: purchasers of the product/service
- a channel audience: suppliers and intermediaries
- any stakeholder with an interest in the organisation's activities (e.g. charities have many stakeholders who may have been affected by the cause represented by the organisation)

When targeting different customers and stakeholders, whether internal or external, or in different market sectors the communications mix needs to be tailored. This means using:

- appropriate communication media and tools to target relevant groups, to suit their needs and characteristics, and to attract them to the message; and

- appropriate modes of communication to express the message in a way that reflects their interests, motives and objectives – and in a way that establishes and maintains constructive, sustainable relationships with them.

Marketers responsible for the delivery of marketing communications need to consider:

- Who should receive the communication
- What the messages should say
- What image of the organisation/brand the stakeholder should retain
- How much resource (financial and personnel) should be invested in the process
- How the message(s) should be delivered

1.2 To differentiate, reinforce, inform and persuade

Marketing communications lie at the heart of the process of developing exchanges between organisations and their customers, and are used to achieve a wide range of marketing objectives. Within this Fill has identified 4 key tasks: to Differentiate, to Reinforce, to Inform and to Persuade: DRIP.

Figure. 1.1 DRIP (Fill, 2006)
With kind permission of Pearson Education Limited: Fill C. (2006) *Simply Marketing Communications*, Financial Times/ Prentice Hall

Differentiate – ensuring that a customer chooses your product or service over that of a competitor means there is a need for clear value to be seen. When there is little to separate a competing product or brand, a value proposition or brand image needs to be created to differentiate your product or service and encourage purchase.

Reinforce – communications may be used to remind people of a need they might have for the offering and the benefits attached to it. It helps customers to relate to it and seek reassurance or comfort that makes them at ease with the exchange. Fill explains that this is important in terms of retaining current customers and building relationships with them, making the relationship more profitable. We will return to this later in this chapter.

Inform – communications need to make customers and prospects aware of an offering, and provide information about the product or service so that they understand the value it offers. There is an educational element.

Persuade – communications may attempt to persuade customers and prospects about the desirability of the offering, and as a consequence to change or continue their behaviour. This might mean making a purchase, trying something new, requesting more information or visiting a website.

So marketing communications can be used to differentiate your brand from your competitors, reinforce positive experience and perceptions of your product or service, educate and inform the market about your offering and persuade customers to buy.

1.3 To build brands

Marketing communications also play a vital role in the development and support of brands and the creation of brand values. They:

- support brand exposure and build awareness;
- communicate the brand values; and
- help to differentiate a brand and give it character.

Communicating the brand effectively means that customers can see how a product is different and understand what a brand stands for and the values it represents. A good brand develops value beyond the physical product.

Brands consist of two main types of attributes: intrinsic and extrinsic (Riezebos, 2002). Intrinsic attributes refer to the functional characteristics of a product such as its shape, performance and physical capacity. If any of these intrinsic attributes were changed, it would directly alter the product.

Promoting the functional aspects usually relies on a *rational* Unique Selling Point (USP). Very often product performance is the focus of the message and a key attribute is identified and used to draw attention to a single superior functional advantage that customers find attractive.

Extrinsic attributes refer to those elements that if changed do not alter the material functioning and performance of the product itself. These might be the brand name, marketing communications, packaging, price and mechanisms that enable consumers to form associations that give meaning to the brand. These attributes help to differentiate one brand from another, and buyers often use the extrinsic attributes to help them distinguish one brand from another especially where it is difficult to make decisions based on the intrinsic (product performance) attributes alone.

Communicating the non-functional aspects rely on an emotional approach. Emotional Selling Points (ESPs) are used to evoke a positive brand association. When an emotional approach is used, product performance characteristics remain in the background while customers are encouraged to develop positive feelings and emotions towards the brand.

A further goal can be to create positive attitudes towards the advertising itself, which in turn can be used to make associations with the brand.

John Lewis
John Lewis has a functional USP in that its price matches its
competition. The 'Never Knowingly Undersold' strap line means that the
consumer knows that they are getting value for money. However, there
is also an emotional brand value that is portrayed through its
advertising of quality products and family values. The brand is not seen
s a budget option but is unlikely to be beaten on price by its
competition.

Visit: www.johnlewis.com

1.4 Supporting the Product Life Cycle

We have already seen that marketing communications can be targeted
at a wide range of different stakeholders and have a range of different
marketing objectives. Another dimension to consider is how marketing
communications need to relate to the Product Life Cycle (PLC). All
products and services, indeed entire organisations and industries, go
through a series of stages as they progress from introduction to their
demise. This is often described as a 'Product Life Cycle' as illustrated in
Figure 1.2.

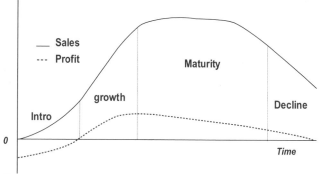

Figure. 1.2 The Product Lifecycle

The value of the PLC model lies in the fact that products and services require a different mix of marketing tools and tactics depending on their stage in the cycle.

There is not room to cover the PLC or the Marketing Mix in full in this Handbook but you can find more about the PLC in the Pricing Handbook and more on the Marketing Mix in Chapter 4.3 and in the Stakeholder Handbook. However, it is worth considering here how marketing communications need to be tailored to the needs of the different stages. Marketing has a place in promoting a product in its infancy, but can be equally as powerful during a product's decline.

With the launch of a new consumer product, it is likely that there will be high initial expenditure on the Promotional Mix. For example, advertising to expose the brand and raise awareness among the target market; and sales promotion to generate trial and purchase. This could be in conjunction with personal selling effort to gain acceptance of the product.

During growth, and as the product matures, it is important to ensure that differential advantage is maintained and that customers know why they should continue to buy your product rather than the competition's offering. This might require activity that builds an image that works over a longer period of time.

The maturity stage is likely to be a defensive or holding operation, since competitors with younger products may be threatening to take customers away. In some cases it might even be a new offering from the same organisation. For example, Apple's iPhone 4 sales will decline in its maturity as customers look to purchase the newer version.

Most consumers know the product exists (apart from a few laggards) and many will have already made a purchase. Consequently, the role of communication is to remind the consumer about the brand image and values, and to provide reassurance that they have chosen the right product.

In the B2B market place, this stage is likely to be about further development and consolidating relationships with customers in preparation for newer products in the portfolio.

Marketing activity may delay the inevitable for a while but it is unlikely to rescue a product that is in decline. The majority of consumers and distributors will have already moved on to newer models and more innovative products. A certain level of advertising and sales promotion might keep models in the market for a while, but eventually even they will drift off. There is little point in diverting resources that could be better used on the next new product.

1.5 Supporting relationship marketing

Of course, communication should not just be one-way. Two-way communication enables organisations to listen to feedback and customer needs, which builds collaborative relationships. Marketing communications is essential to supporting relationship marketing activities. An organisation needs to interact and get feedback from customers so that it can learn and continually add value and service quality.

Organisations need to maintain direct and regular communication through multiple points of contact and across a range of issues, in order to develop valuable relationship ties with all of their stakeholders. Engaging customers in dialogue and developing trust through consistent messages and value propositions provides a basis for building and strengthening stakeholder relationships. Producers need to understand customer motivations if they are to understand their market and be able to 'talk' to them in an effective way.

Relationship marketing seeks to build long-term relationships with selected sufficient-value customers, moving them up the Relationship Marketing Ladder (see Figure 1.3) from prospects to clients and supporters, and eventually to advocates and partners. Each step represents a closer and potentially more profitable relationship for the organisation, and increased value for both parties.

Figure 1.3 The Relationship Marketing Ladder (Christopher et al, 2002)

1.6 Encouraging customer loyalty

Another important objective of marketing communications is to build and maintain customer loyalty. According to the BSi Group: "It costs an organisation at least four times as much to recruit a new customer as to maintain an existing one. Organisations that regularly lose customers, struggle to repair their damaged reputations." (BSI Group, 2013).

Customer retention and loyalty are crucial to any business. Loyalty is not easily gained and organisations frequently become complacent believing they are implementing customer loyalty programmes when, at the very best, they are simply providing mechanisms to buy customer loyalty.

For example, customers very often hold a number of cards from different supermarkets but are not necessarily loyal to any one supermarket. The result is that the 'loyalty' programme did not deliver but many supermarkets feel compelled to have a programme simply to stay competitive.

Customer loyalty towards a brand is built by (Customer Loyalty Institute, 2011):

- regular contact with a customer
- internal marketing that inspires and motivates the workforce to provide a high level of customer service quality
- personalisation and an understanding of individual customers (for example, what they like and do not like)

The Customer Loyalty Grid
The customer loyalty grid developed by Ward shows how customer expectations affect satisfaction, delight and loyalty (Ward, 2013). Ward argues that in order to achieve loyal customers an organisation must meet its customers' expectations and thereby deliver satisfaction.

The aim is to move through the four zones of the grid (there are no short cuts). However, this is not always as easy as it may first appear as not only does the organisation need to ensure it understands what its customers want (their expectations) but customers may not always state what their expectations are, or indeed, even know! This means that good, clear, two way communication is essential.

©2005 - 2013 Affinity Consulting and Training | www.affinitymc.com

Figure 1.4 The Customer Loyalty Grid (Ward, 2013)

In Zone 1: The Zone of Indifference - the aim is to meet customers' very basic needs and wants. These are *expected* and probably not even stated by the customer.
Not meeting them will cause dissatisfaction, achieving them only indifference. You need to understand what these are.

In Zone 2: The Zone of Satisfaction - the customer will tell you what his expectations are – they are still expectations but the customer will articulate this extra requirement. You need to listen as meeting these will lead to satisfaction. Listening is essential to good communication and to achieving loyalty.

In Zone 3: The Zone of Delight - the customer hopes for something, will tell you but does *not expect* it. This is your opportunity to surprise them, to delight them and build the next step towards loyalty.

In Zone 4: The Zone of Loyalty - the aim is to provide benefits that the customer not only does not expect but is not even aware are possible. This is where being innovative, proactive and fully understanding the value of the offering and its potential are key. It results in loyal customers – who may also be willing to pay more for the extra benefits available.

It has been argued that significant financial return can only be achieved through the highest level of loyalty (Hallberg, 2004). It is also important to take into account that there are different types of customer loyalty, and factors that influence loyalty, as illustrated in Figure 1.5 (Fill, 2011).

Emotional loyalty	This is a true form of loyalty and is driven by personal identification with real or perceived values and benefits.
Price loyalty	This type of loyalty is driven by rational economic behaviour, and the main motivations are cautious management of money or financial necessity.
Incentivised loyalty	This refers to promiscuous buyers; those with no favourite brand who need to be encouraged and shown, through repeat experience, the value of becoming loyal.
Monopoly loyalty	This class of loyalty arises where a consumer has no purchase choice owing to a national monopoly. This, therefore, is not a true form of loyalty.

Figure 1.5 Types of loyalty

Marketing communications aimed at building and retaining loyalty need to be different from those used for new business generation. Promotional marketing tools use mass communication with persuasion central to the message. Relationship marketing and improved customer loyalty require interaction and dialogue with individual customers – increasingly through the internet and social media.

1.7 Supporting internal marketing

It is easy to think of marketing communications solely in terms of marketing to external stakeholders. However, in order to maintain a consistent message across all forms of communication and customer touch points, all employees need to understand the organisation's marketing strategy. Internal Marketing is, in effect, the same practice as external communications, only we are trying to engage with our colleagues, rather than the consumer.

Gummesson says: "The objective of internal marketing..... is to create relationships between management and employees, and between functions. The personnel can be viewed as an internal market, and this market must be reached efficiently in order to prepare the personnel for external contacts: efficient internal marketing becomes an antecedent to efficient external marketing." (Gummesson, 2002).

Internal marketing communication is aimed at informing, motivating, rewarding and acknowledging employees with the aims of:

- promoting a marketing orientation and customer awareness throughout the organisation. Gummesson suggests that all employees are in effect 'Part Time Marketers' (Gummesson op. cit.).
- developing the relationship between marketing and other functions in an organisation
- breaking down a 'them and us' culture and gaining buy-in from colleagues
- ensuring brand consistency and consistent messages across all functions of an organisation and touch points with stakeholders
- retaining customers through the delivery of high service quality and increased customer satisfaction
- building a common knowledge and understanding to ensure the organisation is at least as well informed as the customer
- managing and communicating change - achieving a marketing orientation can involve major changes in working practices and organisational culture
- helping employees identify with corporate and marketing objectives

The Marketing Triangle in Figure 1.6 illustrates the importance of internal communication and the interaction between the organisation, its customers and its employees. Kotler suggests that the effectiveness of communication and the likelihood of achieving a sale are diminished if the chain of the triangle is not succinct and if an internal marketing programme is not undertaken before the external one.

This ensures that all employees within the organisation are aware of what is planned and that there is a continuity in marketing messages through employee customer engagement. For example, if customer service employees are not aware of a new marketing offer, then a new enquiry stimulated through marketing will not be dealt with effectively. The consequences of this poorly managed transaction may be that the purchase will not happen at the final stage of the response hierarchy.

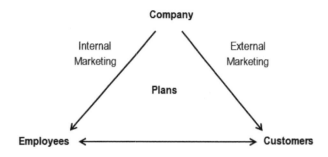

Figure 1.6 The Marketing Triangle

In essence, creating good internal relationships is vital to achieving good relationships with external stakeholders and to ensure that customer engagement is strong at key touch points. It is also worth noting that competitive advantage can be achieved through employee knowledge; product/service innovation can come from employee ideas; and that good customer service needs constant internal reinforcement.

Internal Stakeholder Mapping
As with external stakeholders it is useful to segment internal stakeholders into groups in order to create internal communications which meet different needs.

Internal stakeholders can be segmented into groups by:

- levels of management
- organisational functions
- geographic locations, cultures, etc.

Aubrey Mendelow created a simple model to allow for the mapping of stakeholder interests based on their level of power and their level of interest. If a stakeholder has a high level of interest but low power (e.g. an individual shareholder) they should be kept informed. If on the other hand, they had considerable power, of say an institutional investor, they are deemed to be key to any communications activity. Alternatively, if the stakeholder has low interest but high power (e.g. a watchdog or Sector Regulator, then they must be kept nurtured and kept happy.

An alternative approach suggested by Jobber divides employees into three groups:

- **Supporters** – those who already buy-in to the corporate and marketing objectives of the organisation
- **Neutrals** – those who hold very little opinion, understanding or awareness of the objectives
- **Opposers** – those who disagree with the objectives

The job of internal marketing is to reinforce the backing from Supporters, engage and educate Neutrals, and shift Opposers towards a more supportive position (Jobber, 2007).

Internal marketing tools

There are a number of tools and media that can be used for internal communications including:

- Company reports and accounts
- .Brochures
- Newsletters

- Letters or memos – these may be seen as a rather dated form of communication but letters can provide a confidential and personalised means of communication
- Notice boards
- Corporate intranet
- Email
- Team meetings and briefings – good for two-way communication
- Presentations and conferences
- Training and development programmes
- Video and web-conferencing

Some of these may seem obvious but it is easy to overlook opportunities to reinforce key messages, and alternatives to sending an email. It is just as important in internal marketing as external marketing to select the right tool for the right message and target audience.

Chapter 2: Promotional Tools and Media

When planning its marketing activities, organisations need to consider a number of key issues. These include what is going to be produced, how much is it going to cost, how much is it going to be charged, how the product/service is going to be delivered and how this is going to be communicated to prospects/customers. This is known as the' Marketing Mix', or the 4Ps or 7Ps of marketing: Product, Price, Place, Promotion, People, Processes and Physical Evidence.

2.1 The promotional mix

Promotion, or marketing communications, is one of the original 4Ps of the Marketing Mix. It, in turn, has a range of tools and media and these are known collectively as 'The Promotional Mix'. As with the Marketing Mix the aim is to use the right mix of tools depending on the other elements in both the Promotional and Marketing Mix i.e. to use the right messages and the right promotional tools for the right stakeholders.

There is a wide range of promotional tools and this has grown with the development of the internet and social media.

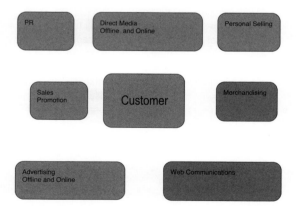

Figure 2.1 The promotional mix

All of these communications tools can be integrated with each other to provide the most effective mix of tools required to engage with all key stakeholders. We will look at each of these key communication tools in turn as well as digital marketing and point of sale marketing.

2.2 Advertising
What is advertising?

Advertising can be defined as any "paid form of non-personal promotion transmitted through a mass medium" (Brassington and Pettitt, 2007). Organisations use advertising to communicate to stakeholders on a large scale relating to a brand message, product or service.

The key difference between advertising and other media in the promotional mix is that it is impersonal and communicates with large numbers of people through paid media channels. It is not personalised to individual stakeholders.

Despite this, advertising can be targeted at segmented market groups through, for example, placement in specialist interest media. The rapid growth of satellite and cable television channels and the internet means that in the digital landscape advertising audiences have become smaller and more niche. This means an advert is far more likely to reach stakeholders with an interest in an organisation's message and a better return on investment can be achieved.

Adverts can be one of two basic types; product-orientated or corporate (Brassington and Pettitt, op.cit.). A corporate advertisement focuses on the institution (and product being offered) to build corporate awareness/ image or values.

In contrast, a product-oriented advert takes one of three alternative forms:

- **Pioneering** – which is used in the early stages of the product lifecycle when it is necessary to explain what the product will do and the benefits it can offer.

- **Competitive** – which is concerned with emphasising any special features of the product or brand or special offers as a way of outselling any competitor offerings.

- **Reminder and reinforcement advertising** – which tends to operate after purchase or further down the product lifecycle as it reminds both prospects and customers that the product still exists and promotes purchase or repeat purchase. This type of advertising also reassures the consumer that they made the right choice in the first place.

Advertising is used to create brand values. Within the marketing mix, advertising also supports other areas of marketing activity. In B2B markets, advertising often directly supports personal and field sales staff by generating leads and the provision of information on new product/service developments. This creates a more receptive environment prior to the sales visit.

Advertising tools
Advertising can be in print or digital form and communicated through the following media:

- **TV** – probably the most expensive form to create and place but, excellent at reaching large audiences. In recent years there has been a significant proliferation of TV channels with smaller audiences but enabling better segmentation and targeting. Organisations can also sponsor TV programmes and on some channels use Product Placement to reinforce advertisements.

However, with the advent of on-demand television and hard drives television adverts can be fast-forwarded making it more difficult to ensure that they are actually viewed. TV audience figures can be found from the Broadcasters Audience Research Board (BARB) at: http://www.barb.co.uk.

- **Radio** – audio advertising is available on many commercial radio stations, some nationally but predominantly on a more local geographic basis. The growth of digital radio and fragmentation of new stations has also opened up the opportunity for better segmentation and targeting. In addition the current boom in internet radio has created 100s if not 1000s of new channels for advertising on a local, national and international scale, and enabled audio advertising to be backed up with website content. However, the audiences of these channels can be small. Audio adverts are cheaper to produce and place than the video required for TV or cinema but have less impact. Information on radio stations and audiences can be found from the Radio Joint Audience Research (RAJAR) at: http://www.rajar.co.uk and the Radio Advertising Bureau (RAB) at: http://www.rab.co.uk.

- **Cinema** – amazingly the first cinema advert in the UK appeared in 1899 – an advert for Dewars Whisky. It was silent! Contrast this with the first ever sound activated cinema advert trialled in 2012 (Baker, 2012). Cinema adverts benefit from a high level of video and audio impact and creativity and can be highly targeted alongside the target audience for a film; and cinema numbers have increased dramatically over the last 10 years. However, this medium suffers from high creation costs for good quality video relative to the audience size reached. Information on cinema audiences can be found from the Cinema Exhibitors' Association (CEA) at: http://www.cinemauk.org.uk.

- **Print media** – includes local, regional, national and international (e.g. the Financial Times), free (Metro) and paid-for newspapers; and trade and consumer magazines.

Within both newspapers and magazines there are 2 distinct types of advertising: standard 'display' adverts which can be placed in colour or black and white, with the size and positioning specified; and 'classified' adverts which are more concise, constrained to specific sections and sold by the column inch. Print adverts are relatively cheap compared to audio and video (although a full page colour advert in The Times currently costs over £27,000 - costs are easy to find on all publications' websites). They can also be highly targeted using readership profiles, have a longer 'shelf life' and can be seen many times over as most print media have a higher 'readership' than 'circulation' figure i.e. more than one person reads each copy. Circulation and readership profiles can be found from the National Readership Survey (NRS) at: http://www.nrs.co.uk and the Audit Bureau of Circulation (ABC) at: http://www.abc.org.uk.

- **Digital** – the rise of the internet has provided many new opportunities for advertising. Initially the focus was on banner advertising on websites but today this sector has morphed into a much wider, digital version of all off-line media as people spend more and more time online. Digital advertising opportunities include:

    o online magazines and newspapers
    o websites, phones and tablets
    o online games
    o mobile Apps
    o interactive adverts
    o SMS (short message service) – text messaging
    o Social Media - many organisations now use Facebook and other social media such as LinkedIn and Twitter not just as part of their social media strategy but also for advertising

○ 'Pay PER Click' (PPC), which is one of the most common methods of advertising on the internet. An advert placed will appear at the top of a set of Search Engine rankings and payment is made for every viewer who clicks on the advert through to the advertiser's website.

You can find more about these and other digital marketing techniques in Sections 2.8 and 2.9.

- **Outdoors** – this is usually in the form of posters on billboards (or hoardings), bus stops, buses, trains, etc. Some are now digital and interactive e.g. incorporating a QR Code which can be scanned by a smartphone providing instant additional information or a link.

Advertising today

In relation to DRIP (Figure 1.1), advertising can be used to differentiate, reinforce, inform and persuade audiences. However, apart from its ability to reach large audiences, the key strengths of advertising have been to develop corporate and product brand awareness, values and associations. Now in the digital world and with the growth of interactive communication, marketers are increasingly including a 'call-to-action' in their advertising to encourage a behavioural response.

It is also important to note that, in the past, advertising campaigns were often created and managed using one medium. Today the emphasis is on integration and co-ordination between media and over time.

Further information

Most media suppliers will provide 'media packs' detailing the size and characteristics of their market audience as well as costs. You can obtain more information on advertising facts and figures from: World Advertising Research Centre (WARC): www.warc.com; OfCom: www.ofcom.org.uk and Route: www.outdoormediacentre.org.uk

2.3 Public relations
What is public relations?

The Chartered Institute of Public Relations defines public relations (PR) as "about reputation – the result of what you do, what you say and what others say about you" (CIPR, 2011).

PR is a relatively low cost and effective way of communicating a message to a wide number of audiences, referred to as 'publics', and raising an organisation's profile. It is a discipline that looks after reputation with the aim of earning understanding and support, and influencing opinion and behaviour. It is a planned and sustained effort to establish and maintain good will and mutual understanding between an organisation and its publics. PR is not only useful when you have something good to say, but can also be useful in terms of managing a crisis.

As Fill states: "The increasing use of public relations, and in particular publicity, is a reflection of the high credibility attached to this form of communication" (Fill, *op. cit.*).

Historically, the core of public relations - media relations - includes all efforts to publicise products or the company to members of the press including TV, radio, newspapers, magazines and the internet. In garnering media coverage, PR professionals work with the media to place stories about their products and company. This is achieved by developing interesting and relevant story angles that are pitched to the media. It is important to remember that media placements come with good stories and no payment is made to the media for them.

PR and media relations tools

A good PR campaign will focus on the media that an organisation's publics use.

The key tools used include:

- **Press packs** – these can include written information such as a news release, background information about an organisation, key spokesperson biographies and other supporting materials. Online press rooms can be used to cater to media needs and provide instant information.

- **News or press releases** – these can be disseminated on a small to mass scale to multiple but relevant publications and media outlets. They tend to be reasonably short and editors will choose whether to publish them based on their news worthiness.

- **Audio or video news releases** – these are pre-recorded features distributed to news media that may be included within media programming.

- **Feature articles** – these are agreed in principle with a word count before being written. They may be written by the PR team or by a reporter, conducting interviews and research in conjunction with the PR function. The best possible outcome is that the reporter or editor will write a positive story with the company as a key feature or, at least include the company's name somewhere within an industry-focused article. Many publications will publish 'Forward Feature' lists for content they want and article placement can be agreed through an Editor or Features Editor.

- **Advertorials** – these are a cross between an advert and an article. Usually, advertorials are paid for spaces that feature a visual with larger amounts of content. Quite often adverts can be accompanied by editorial negotiated as part of agreeing advertising expenditure. Advertorials must be clearly identified.

- **Newsletters** – these can be directed at trade customers, final consumers or business buyers and can be distributed either by regular mail or electronically using RSS feeds or email (the latter providing the opportunity to include links for information or purchase). Good newsletters should provide content of interest to customers as well as information on products and promotions e.g. a bookstore may include reviews of new books and information about online book chats as well as in-store or online promotions. Effective newsletters are sought out by and well received by interested audiences.

- **Insight** – focus groups, panel discussions or debates can provide interesting PR coverage, as can market research, which may provide statistics and insight that can form a feature article.

- **Event Management** – these can range from receptions to elegant dinners to stunts such as world record attempts that can capture wide media attention. Special events can be designed to reach a specific narrow target audience. Care needs to be taken to ensure the event conveys the correct message for the target audience and image of the organisation and brand.

- **Speaking Engagements** – Speaking before industry conventions, trade association meetings and other groups provides an opportunity for company experts to demonstrate their expertise to potential clients/customers. Generally these opportunities are not explicitly for company or product promotion; rather they are a chance to talk on a topic of interest to potential customers and serve to highlight the speaker's expertise in a field. Often the only mention of the company or its products is in the speaker biography. Nevertheless, the right speaking engagement puts the company in front of a good target audience and offers networking opportunities for generating customer leads.

- **Sponsorship** – organisations and brands use sponsorships to build goodwill and brand recognition by associating with an event or group. Marketers can examine sponsorship opportunities to find those that reach target groups, fit within a specified budget and reflect appropriate product or brand values. There are numerous local, regional, national and international sponsorship opportunities, for example major cultural or sporting events like the London 2012 Olympic Games. Most organisations seeking company sponsors provide information on the variety of sponsorship levels available including data on event audience, exposure opportunities (signage, promotional items, public announcements, receptions, conference speaking opportunities, etc.).

- **Lobbying** – is the practice of individuals and organisations trying to influence the opinions and decisions of government officials, MPs and Lords. Methods of lobbying vary and can range from sending letters and making presentations to providing briefing material to Members and organising rallies. Lobbying can be very influential and there are professional lobbyists who can be hired. However, final decisions are, of course, ultimately down to the official or MP who may have many other influences to take into account.

- **Corporate social responsibility (CSR) and community relations** – CSR has become a key issue for many organisations and can be used effectively as part of a PR campaign to promote an organisation's corporate image. CSR programmes may be environmental, ethical, charitable or social but should be relevant to the company's business, values and mission. In addition for many companies, fostering good relations with key audiences includes building strong relationships with their local community.

- **Blogs** – blogs are usually informal opinion pieces posted online. Some blogs have large numbers of followers and allow readers to leave comments. In that sense, blogging can be seen as a form of social networking. Indeed, bloggers do not only produce content to post on their blogs but also build social relations with their readers and other bloggers. Other forms of blogging include; art blogs, photoblogs, video blogging and podcasting.

- **Social Media** – as with advertising the use of social media has grown hugely as a PR tool. Using Facebook, LinkedIn, Twitter, etc to communicate quickly, frequently and informally with stakeholders gives organisations exciting opportunities to communicate PR messages and gain feedback.

PR as a communications tool

All stakeholders, (customers, suppliers, employees and investors), can have a powerful impact and so can journalists and regulators.
They all have an opinion about the organisations they come into contact with. Whether these are good, bad, right or wrong, an organisation's reputation can change in the public perception very quickly. In the long term, these perceptions will drive buying decisions.

Reputation, along with a value proposition, provides a competitive edge. Effective PR can help manage reputation by communicating and building good relationships with all of an organisation's stakeholders. The media can affect the way its readers, an organisation's clients, make decisions, and a proactive and focused media programme can influence the way journalists present the news.

PR works best when used for two-way communication. Although primarily used to tell the organisation's story, through research, feedback and evaluation, PR practitioners can find out the concerns and expectations of a company's publics and explain them to its management.

Grunig & Hunt identify four models of PR which illustrate the different approaches to disseminating information(Grunig & Hunt, 1984). The following diagram is adapted from Grunig & Hunt with kind permission from James E Grunig.

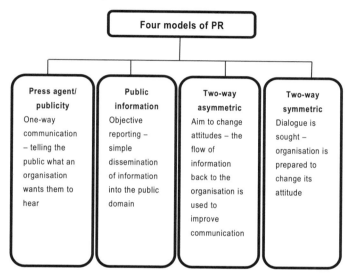

Figure 2.2 Four models of PR (Grunig & Hunt, 1984)

PR can be both a tactical and strategic tool. It could be said that PR offers only a short-term impact, however, the immediate effect of PR allows follow-up advertising to have more of an impact. If you see an advert you see the content but if you read an article you are more likely to believe the content of the advertisement.

One advantage that PR does have over advertising is cost, as it tends to be very cost-effective. Although many organisations outsource their PR, essentially the major cost is time.

It is also important to remember that it is difficult to control a message once it has been issued, but third-party endorsement can be more influential and have a greater impact on a target audience than any of the other tools in the communications mix.

Further information
You can obtain more information on PR including best practice guides and case studies from the CIPR at: www.cipr.co.uk.

2.4 Sales promotion

Traditionally, sales promotions have been tactical techniques designed to add value to a product or service over and above the normal product offering. They are a 'call to action' and use special short-term techniques to persuade members of a target market to respond or undertake certain activity. As a reward, marketers offer something of value to those responding, generally in the form of a lower purchase price, money back, etc. or the inclusion of additional value-added material, for example, buy-one-get-one-free offers, a free sample, gift or entry into a prize draw.

Sales promotions are often confused with advertising. However, what distinguishes sales promotion is that it involves a short-term value proposition and that the customer must perform some activity in order to be eligible to receive the value proposition (advertising often includes a sales promotion). The inclusion of a timing constraint (e.g. promotion end-date) and an activity requirement (e.g. redeeming a coupon) are typical of sales promotions.

Sales promotion has the capability to communicate with the customer in ways that advertising struggles to emulate. Advertising can tell people that a product is 'new, improved', or that it offers certain features and benefits, but this is conceptual information, which people may not fully understand or accept. Sales promotion can put a product sample into people's hands so they can experience it for themselves, which is more powerful and convincing.

Sales promotion is primarily a tool for accelerating sales. However, there are a number of other objectives including:

- attracting new customers
- retaining existing customers
- rewarding existing customers
- increasing quantities purchased
- encouraging repeat purchases
- defending shelf space in supermarkets
- encouraging distributors and retailers to stock the product
- tackling 'seasonality' - infrequent and fluctuating sales can be countered by sales promotions

Loyalty incentives

Perhaps the main problem with the traditional definition of sales promotion is that, with the development of relationship marketing techniques, there is now more emphasis on building long-term relationships with consumers. Consequently, marketers are now looking for ways of developing the scope of traditional sales promotion to encourage long-term loyalty, retention and repeat purchasing. Loyalty schemes, such as supermarket loyalty cards, are sales promotions in the sense that they offer added value over and above the normal product offering, but they are certainly not short-term tactical measures – quite the opposite.

Sales promotion techniques: consumers

Consumer promotion techniques include:

- Price promotions through discounted selling prices, additional product(s) on current purchase, buy-one-get-one-free ('BOGOF') offers, coupons or discounts on future purchases
- Free samples or trial size offers to tempt new customers
- Gifts with a purchase or premium promotions, where the customer receives a bonus, gift or refund with a purchase or repeat purchase
- Competitions and prizes, for example, prize draws are often used to stimulate sales and to capture customer data

Sales promotion techniques: channel management

Intermediaries provide a vital service for the manufacturer in the distribution, stocking and display of goods. Some intermediaries, for example, major supermarkets which have significant power in channel management, might expect or insist on sales promotions before they will co-operate with any manufacturer demands.

Trade promotions are predominantly about gaining more product penetration, more display and more promotional effort on the part of the distributor. There can be conflict between the parties because of their different priorities and objectives and consequently the manufacturer may need to provide an extremely attractive incentive (Fill, 2011). This is also further complicated by the competition with other manufacturers and their products. Demand for shelf space puts the power back in the hands of the intermediary who will be looking for the most attractive incentives and value for their customers, as well as return for them.

New product launches have to be considered carefully. The launch period, as has been discussed in terms of the product lifecycle, is a key time. If the distribution and channel management is weak then sales could be disastrous. If a manufacturer does not get the sales promotion strategy of a new product right then consumers (especially early adopters) are not going to have immediate access to purchase the product.

For the intermediary, there is the risk of a new product not selling and having a lot of stock to sell. Trade promotions, especially those with a push strategy (see Chapter Five) can reduce some of this risk. Money-based promotions help to reduce the potential financial loss from a product failure but this must be balanced against the positioning and brand strategy adopted – or these could be devalued.

Further information

The Institute of Promotional Marketing (IPM): www.theipm.org.uk

2.5. Personal selling

Not all communication between an organisation and its customers can be effected through advertising or digital marketing effort. The human touch still has a role to play.

Personal selling using a one-to-one sales strategy that involves sales staff or account managers to represent an organisation, has real value especially in B2B marketing and with complex, high-value, low quantity products and services.

A well trained salesperson who understands the product or service, its brand image, and the benefits or value it offers to the customer, can also be a very effective promotional tool. Personal selling enables two-way communication, can provide instant response to customer queries, enable a fuller understanding of the customer's requirements, and build effective longer-term relationships.

On the downside it is a high cost approach – with a human resource cost in terms of time, salary and commission and relatively low reach. In addition, marketers do not have as much control over the messages delivered or the image of the organisation conveyed. In reacting to a new situation, the sales people may advertently or inadvertently communicate different messages.

Discounting can be a particular issue and it is essential that sales staff know whether discounts may be offered or not and there are legal implications as promises made by the salesperson are covered by Marketing Communications law.

These problems mean that a consistent value proposition may not be executed. Of course by doing this, the sale may still be achieved but at a cost.

Further information

The Institute of Sales and Marketing Management (ISMM):
www.ismm.co.uk

2.6. Direct marketing

There are many different approaches to direct marketing including traditional offline methods such as mail shots, leaflet drops, mail order catalogues, direct response advertising and telemarketing; and electronic methods such as email, SMS (short message service) and social media. The most appropriate for an organisation will depend on the brand, the stakeholder, the messages and the responses desired. The main aim of direct marketing is to establish a personal relationship between the organisation and the stakeholder.

Direct mail and electronic direct mail

Direct mail can be defined as personally addressed advertising. Originally, these were postal mailings, which could be personalised and targeted, but this has now developed into electronic direct mail i.e. personalised and targeted emails. Similarly mail order catalogues are distributed both by post and online as well as being available in-store.

Direct mail is still one of the most popular methods used. It is widely believed to be one of the most effective in generating leads and enquiries and in achieving a sale. Using an up to date and well-targeted mailing list is key. Personalised messages and information about products and services can be sent directly to people who may be interested in it. On the downside direct mail can often be mistaken for junk mail, but if planned correctly, it can be highly effective in both business and consumer markets.

Leaflet drops, inserts and handouts

Leaflet drops can be undertaken by an organisation's sales team or by an agent who delivers them door-to-door. More usually, however, the Royal Mail is paid to distribute them with the post. Inserts can be included in newspapers and magazines via the publisher, or on a more local scale, a newsagent can be used to distribute with a newspaper or magazine. Another example may be handing out leaflets and flyers to delegates at an event, exhibition or conference.

Although similar to direct mail, these are cheaper but not as effective. Response rates are lower, even though the content and quality can be the same, because they are not personalised or as well targeted. It is a lead generation tool that will probably be looking for a direct response from the recipient. The main aims again being to raise awareness and trigger an enquiry or sale.

Direct response advertising

Direct response advertising is designed to elicit an immediate response from customers – ranging from an enquiry to a sale. Direct Response advertising may be in direct mail or leaflets – looking for a reply card or response coupon to be completed and returned, may be online ('click here now'), or may be on the radio or TV with an advert giving a telephone number, website or facebook details for the response. TV has, of course, also evolved into interactive TV through the 'red button', giving viewers the option of transferring to more information, and through the proliferation of 'home shopping' channels.

Direct response advertising has a number of advantages – it can prompt quick (time limited) responses, collects information about the respondent, and can be readily measured in terms of effectiveness (number of coupons returned/ number of calls received).

SMS/text marketing

Text messaging grew rapidly in line with the huge growth in mobile phone use and became a highly attractive direct marketing tool.

It has a number of advantages over traditional marketing methods including:

- mailing to large groups quickly
- mobile phone users tend to take their phone with them, which makes it easier to reach them with time-sensitive messages
- people tend to read every message they get, which means it is far less likely to be ignored than emails, door-drop leaflets, etc.

However, there are strict privacy, data protection and e-commerce rules that must be complied with. In addition the nature of text messaging means that content is restricted; and similarly to telemarketing, there can be a sense of invasion of privacy.

With the growth of electronic devices such as smart phones and tablets, text messaging is not as popular as it once was.

Telemarketing

Contacting potential customers by telephone can offer a number of advantages over other forms of marketing including:

- gauging a customer's interest immediately;
- asking questions to assess a customer's individual requirements; and
- explaining technical or complex messages more effectively.

However, there are also significant disadvantages, including the obvious annoyance people find with cold calling. In particular in the B2C marketplace, receiving unsolicited phone calls at home can be a great irritation. In B2B marketing, people are more receptive to marketing calls as part of their work; however, telemarketers are often still met with a negative attitude. There are strict rules on who can be contacted by telephone.

Telemarketing is not just a sales tool, but can also be used for undertaking market research, customer service and account management. It is generally used to:

- build databases
- generate leads and appointments
- follow up responses to direct-mail campaigns
- keep in touch with customers and renew relationships with lapsed customers, and
- find out about industry developments and the activities of competitors.

Further information

The Direct Marketing Association (DMA): www.dma.org.uk

2.7 Point of sale merchandising

Another important communication tool is merchandising i.e. packaging, labelling and visual display at the point of purchase which backs up the brand values communicated by advertising.

For many small-to-medium organisations, particularly in an economic downturn, budget cutbacks mean that advertising funds are not available to develop the brand identity and they have turned increasingly to merchandising to promote the brand.

Whether backed up by advertising or not it is essential that all merchandising and point of sale marketing is consistent both with the brand image and any other promotional activities being undertaken.

2.8 Opinion leaders and formers

We have already discussed the importance of relationship marketing and building trust. Another key tool for marketing communications is to use opinion leaders and formers as brand advocates and generate word of mouth communication.

Opinion leaders are 'ordinary' people to whom others look for information and advice. They are 'early adopters' of new ideas and seek out information which they pass on to family, friends, work colleagues and social groups – increasingly today using social media. They may sometimes be used in advertisements to aid credibility.

Opinion formers are people who are considered to be knowledgeable or an expert. As a result their advice is credible and through reviews, recommendations and endorsement they can help support a marketing message. Opinion formers can raise the profile of various social issues because of their position in society e.g. Bono, Bob Geldof, Chris Martin and a range of others within the entertainment industry.

Messages delivered by attractive sources achieve higher retention recall. Organisations regularly use celebrities to act as a spokesperson to endorse their products. However, this is only effective for as long as the celebrity is seen as being both an expert and/or trustworthy in the public perception. Accenture had a partnership with the golfer Tiger Woods which, once his marriage problems became huge international news, was terminated. He was no longer a credible opinion former in the public domain.

The three factors most often identified as crucial to becoming a trusted opinion former are:

- **Expertise** – specialised knowledge giving credibility to the information and claims communicated. For example, doctors and scientists.
- **Trustworthiness** – how objective and honest the source is perceived to be.
- **Likeability** – the source's attractiveness to the audience. Qualities such as openness, humour and being natural will make a source more likeable. Celebrities usually score highly for likeability.

2.9 Digital marketing

We have already touched on digital advertising but the rise in new technology and interactive services has led to so many new media tools and new and exciting ways to communicate with stakeholders that it is worth looking at some of these in more detail. Digital marketing includes online advertising, websites, email marketing, affiliate marketing, remarketing and social media such as Facebook, Twitter, LinkedIn and Pinterest.

The benefits of digital technology include added impact, speed and interactivity. So, for example, combining copy, audio and video in an email or on a website (instead of sending a conventional mail shot), having interactive point of sale displays in stores, using social media to connect with millions of people and potentially creating something so immediate and innovative that it goes 'viral'!

Banner advertising

A web banner, or banner ad, is an advertisement placed on a web page. It is intended to attract web traffic from that website to the advertiser's site. The advertisement is usually constructed from an image and can feature animation, sound or video to maximise impact.

These adverts are usually placed on web pages that have interesting content, such as a newspaper article or an opinion piece.

Similar to traditional advertising, where an advert is placed in a relevant trade publication, an organisation would tend to place an advert on a website visited by key stakeholders or with relevant visitor demographics. The owner of the website on which the advert is placed is known as an 'affiliate' and for every unique user that clicks on the advert, the affiliate earns money. This is known as affiliate marketing. Alternatively, advertising rates, similar to those of rate cards in newspapers and magazines are employed.

Pay-Per-Click (PPC)
Pay per click (PPC), also known as cost per click, is an internet advertising model used to direct traffic to websites, where advertisers pay the publisher (typically a website owner or search engine like Google) when the advert is clicked. With search engines, advertisers typically bid on keyword phrases relevant to their target market. Content sites commonly charge a fixed price per click rather than use a bidding system.

PPC also implements an affiliate model. The affiliates provide purchase-point click-through to a website. It is a pay-for-performance model; if an affiliate does not generate click-throughs it represents no cost to the advertiser. As a result, it is a cost-effective method.

Websites that utilise PPC ads will display an advertisement when a keyword query matches an advertiser's keyword list, or when a content site displays relevant content. Such advertisements are called 'sponsored links' or 'sponsored ads' and appear adjacent to or above organic results on search engine results pages, or anywhere a web developer chooses on a content site.

Although Google Adwords is the most commonly known PPC provider, it is not the only option. Yahoo! Search Marketing, and Microsoft adCenter are similar operators and all operate a bid-based model.

Search Engine Optimisation (SEO)

Although not a communications tool per se SEO is another important concept for marketers. It is the process of improving the visibility of a website or a web page in search engines via an unpaid or organic approach. In other words optimising a website so that when users search for keywords, your organisation is better matched and more likely to appear higher in search engine lists, ideally on the first page. Generally, the higher the ranking a website has on the search results page, the more frequently it will be visited.

SEO may target different kinds of search, including image search, local search, video search, academic search, news search and industry-specific vertical search engines.

Location-based marketing

Location-based marketing is the technique of using global-positioning technology to send geographic-specific marketing to consumers over their mobile devices. Location-based marketing allows brands to adapt their marketing messages based on where consumers are geographically when they see the messages, and also what that location may tell you about them.

The growth of the smart phone has provided a number of opportunities for brands to engage with consumers based on their current location. Whether by developing mobile apps or creating text message-based marketing campaigns, businesses can tailor their offers to combine a consumer's interests and location in order to drive traffic to their websites.

Foursquare

Foursquare is a location-based social networking website for mobile devices. Originally it enabled registered users to post their location at a particular venue on social media sites and link up with friends. Subsequently Foursquare Brands was developed which enables users to receive special information and 'tips' from companies when they check-in at certain locations and 'follow' the company. In 2012 Foursquare launched an App update called 'Promoted Updates' which allows companies to issue messages to Foursquare users about relevant deals or available products. There are currently over 35 million users. Go to: www.foursquare.com for more information.

Remarketing

Remarketing allows an organisation to show ads to viewers who have previously visited its website as they continue to browse the internet. By placing cookies on the viewer's PC and using specific tags an advertiser can 'follow' a visitor once they leave their own website. Websites must declare when they are using cookies.

So, for example if the searcher visited your website to search for a particular TV and then move on to look at TVs elsewhere, your advertisement can appear on the search engine pages and on other websites which allow advertising. The great advantage here, apart from reinforcement, is that the advert (in terms of both product and message) can be very targeted at people with a known interest.

Social media

Social media marketing refers to the process of gaining website traffic or attention through social media sites. Social media is a relationship marketing tool that helps to engage with stakeholders and encourage communication, comment and word of mouth.

A message, thread or product spreads from user to user and resonates because it appears to come from a trusted, third-party source, as opposed to the brand or company itself.

Hence, this form of marketing is driven by 'word-of-mouth', meaning it results in earned media rather than paid media.

Social media has become a platform that is easily accessible to anyone with internet access. Increased communication for organisations encourages brand awareness and often, improved customer service. Additionally, social media are a relatively inexpensive platform for organisations to implement marketing campaigns. Like most digital media its effectiveness can also be easily measured.

Social networking websites allow individuals to interact with one another and build relationships. When brands or companies join those sites, people can interact with the brand or company. That interaction feels personal to users because of their previous experiences with social networking site interactions.

Social networking sites like Twitter, Facebook, Google+, YouTube, Pinterest and blogs allow individual followers to 'retweet' or 'repost' comments made by the organisation.

By repeating the message, all of the user's connections are able to see the message, and so it reaches many more people. In this way social media can attract new customers as well as build and reinforce loyalty among current customers.

The increased popularity of mobile phones has only benefited social media usage. Tablets and smart phones with social networking capabilities mean customers are constantly online and have a real-time experience. This easy connection to social networking sites means the user is constantly reminded and updated about brands, their capabilities, uses, importance, values, etc.

In the context of the social web, engagement means that customers and stakeholders are participants rather than viewers. Social media in business allows anyone and everyone to express and share an opinion or idea somewhere along the business's path to market.

Each participating customer becomes part of the marketing department, as other customers read their comments or reviews. The engagement process is then fundamental to successful social media marketing and this is key to building relationships and brand loyalty.

Social media has dramatically changed the landscape for word-of-mouth. It is a personal environment, a group, a place of belonging. People trust the word of friends and associates much more than advertising messages; they are far more likely to act on a recommendation from a friend than an organisation.

2.10 Effective marketing communications

As we have seen there is a wide range of communication tools available to the marketer. Different elements of the marketing communications mix reach stakeholders through different media, communicating in different ways to help marketers achieve different objectives.
It is essential to select the right media for the right message for the right audience and all of these decisions need to be right for the brand.

For example, advertising is good for generating awareness, whereas personal selling is more effective at promoting action and purchase behaviour. Because the tools within the marketing mix are more effective in different ways, a mix can produce complementary results.

And, especially in today's digital world, any campaign that can harness the use of personal recommendation effectively, is more likely to be successful (Fill, op. cit.).

Table 2.1 below provides a summary of the advantages and disadvantages of the key communication tools:

Communications Tools	Pros	Cons
TV	• Easy to reach a wide audience as the vast majority of the population has access to television. • You can choose which channels to advertise on depending on your target market, e.g. a children's product on the CBBC channel. • You can demonstrate your product and its uses and add a factor of entertainment.	• Viewing habits have changed greatly in the past ten years as new technology has become available. Many viewers are now able to record their television programmes and therefore skip the adverts. • The production costs and costs of placement are high.
Radio	• Can reach an audience on a national, regional or local basis depending on your target market. • The advertisements can be repeated which can drill your message into the minds of potential customers. • Tends to be cheaper than TV or print.	• It is difficult to ensure that radio listeners are paying attention to your ads, especially if they are listening whilst performing another task such as driving.
Cinema	• The dramatic effects that are specific to a cinema such as the surround sound and atmosphere are features which can benefit your advertisement. • The audience cannot fast forward the advert. • You can choose which films to broadcast your advert alongside depending on your target audience.	• Very costly, especially if you want your advertisement played before a well-hyped blockbuster. • Many people do not pay attention to the ads and use the time to buy popcorn or go to the toilet instead of watching them.

Newspapers (Print Media)	• Newspapers are considered trustworthy sources. • Although the number of people who use newspapers as their primary source of information has fallen over the past few decades, it still provides a large potential audience. • Can choose specific newspapers for your advertisements to target specific markets.	• Large ad spaces are costly and for the length of time that the newspaper will be on offer, it may not be a worthy investment. • Newspapers are filled with ads - yours may not stand out.

Magazines (Print Media)	• Specific magazines are directed at different target audiences which makes reaching your target audience an easier task. • Magazines tend to have a longer life than newspapers as they are left in waiting rooms or at the hairdressers.	• Deadlines are often needed months in advance which can mean a long wait before reaping the benefits of your ad and it can be difficult to ensure the ad coincides with the arrival of a new product. • Magazines are filled with ads - yours may not stand out.
Outdoors	• Likely to reach many consumers as there is no limitation on how many consumers it is exposed to. • Low cost.	• Public tend to give outdoor advertising a low level of attention. • Exposure can be fleeting e.g. posters on buses can drive by with no time for the consumer to read it.

PR	• Generates product awareness and reaches an audience which may otherwise not have come into contact with your brand. • Speaking engagements provide an opportunity to interact with potential customers to help generate sales. • People perceive sponsorship as a good deed which portrays the company in a positive light and presents a good public image for the brand.	• Difficult to measure the impact of PR and its effect on sales. • Can be difficult to maintain a 'win-win' situation for both the sponsors and those being sponsored to feel the benefits of the partnership and be satisfied with it.

Sales Promotion	• Attracts new customers who may not have come into contact with the company or product otherwise. • Can be used to generate quick revenue.	• If this strategy is used too often, customers can start to expect the lower price to remain a constant and therefore show reluctance to buy the product at a higher price. • Although used to create quick profits, this is not a strategy for use in the long-term. • It can undermine the value of the brand.
Personal Selling	• The face-to-face interaction can help to improve customer relationships. • Communication and approach can be personalised. • There is an opportunity to close the sale; a successful sales representative can convert an interested customer into a buyer.	• Labour intensive. • The reach of customers is limited; can only reach customers who have already sought information or entered the store.

Direct Mail and Electronic Direct Mail	• Mail can be personalised to suit the different target segments with no risk of the message being misrepresented. • Mail materials are relatively cheap to produce. • Customers can read their mail when and if they want to rather than feeling pressured to. • Email can reach large numbers cheaply.	• The response to direct mail is very small (1%). • Need to ensure addresses are up-to-date; need a good customer relationship management system. • Emails can be easily ignored/may irritate.

Leaflet drops, Inserts and Handouts	• Leaflets and flyers are cheap to produce. • You can choose which geographical segments to target.	• Need to find people willing to take on the job of delivering the advertisements to the public. • Need to pay for employee labour. • Easy to ignore.
Direct Response Advertising	• Direct communication with customers allows for more personalised interaction. • Fast response from consumers allows for effective time management. • Easy to measure effectiveness of advertising.	• Can be difficult to find people willing to provide a response.
SMS/Text Marketing	• Quick and easy to reach large numbers of people. • The number of people with a mobile phone is high so there is a large target audience.	• Consumers can feel an invasion of their privacy, especially if they did not willingly give out their phone number. • Many texts will be deleted as soon as it is recognised that the message is sales.

Telemarketing	• Low levels of effort and money needed compared to that needed for face-to-face marketing. • Pre-recorded answer machine messages save the need for a calling team.	• The odds of getting through to someone who is willing to listen are small; most get through to an answer machine or someone who is not willing to talk which can be disheartening for employees. • Consumers tend not to trust the information provided to them by cold callers. • Connections usually need to be made between the caller and prospect before making a sale which can be time-consuming.
Point of Sale Merchandising	• Customers who are at the point of sale are already interested in buying your products from you. • If there is a queue, customers are forced to spend time looking at your products and consider whether or not they are worth buying.	• The products on display need to be well considered; customers are not likely to buy expensive, high value items on impulse. • Quality must meet the brand values.
Opinion Leaders and Formers	• Can be very influential. • Selected expert can be well matched to target market. • Generated Word of Mouth is cheap and can be very powerful.	• Opinion leaders are hard to control. • Paid experts/celebrities can be expensive and can have a negative effect if their reputation becomes tarnished.
Banner Advertising	• Internet banners can be highly visible. • The number of people with access to the internet worldwide is huge (2.5 billion in 2013) so the exposure potential is large.	• Hard to measure how effective your banner is. Even if consumers are visiting a website which has your banner advertised, that does not mean they have read it or paid it any kind of attention. • Many consider website

		banners to be irritating.
Pay-Per-Click (PPC)	• Cost efficient; you only pay when a customer clicks on your ad. • PPC advertisements are quick to implement and easy to set up. • You can choose where the ad appears and choose what it says to maximise clicks.	• You have to pay for all clicks, even if they do not turn into a sale. • People are most trusting of, and therefore more likely to click on 'organic' results, rather than those which are sponsored.

Search Engine Optimisation (SEO)	• People are most trusting of, and therefore more likely to click on 'organic' results, rather than those which are sponsored. • A high ranking in major search engines suggests that you are also likely to appear in the majority of the search engines worldwide.	• Changes to the website can be costly and time consuming. • There is no certainty that you will rank highly amongst the search engines.
Location-based marketing	• Can be well targeted and relevant. • Efficient use of resources as there is no risk of spending time and money on advertising to those whose geographical location affects their view on a product, e.g. advertising McDonalds in India.	• By segmenting by location, there is a risk of isolating potential customers. • Can be irritating and intrusive.

Remarketing	• Easy to implement. • Remarketing cookies allow you to target your audience in different ways by changing the message presented in your ads based on who is seeing them, e.g. a different message to someone who has bought your product online before compared to someone who left the site without a purchase.	• Some see cookies as a method of being 'hounded' and can create bad feelings towards a company.
Social Media	• As of 2013, there were 1.11 billion people with Facebook accounts and over 200 million active accounts on Twitter; a huge target audience for your brand and its message. • Can receive quick feedback through direct contact with customers. • The cost of entry is low; it is extremely quick, easy and free to create a profile on Facebook or Twitter.	• There is a large risk of negative backlash if profiles are not managed carefully. • Managing a profile can be time-consuming as the brand must maintain a 'voice' that communicates regularly with its audience and respond to queries on a daily basis.

Table 2.1 The Pros and Cons of different promotional tools

Chapter 3: Building and Supporting Brands

As we have already seen in Chapter 1, one of the key objectives of marketing communications is to build and support brands. In this chapter we look at how key marketing communications tools can be used to achieve this.

3.1 Building and supporting brands

Broadcast advertising – supports brand development through its constant repetition of the brand name and reinforcement of the brand characteristics in the consumer's mind. This is especially important in highly competitive markets such as cosmetics. Brand consistency across all advertising helps distinguish an organisation's product. Public associations with a brand are key and consistent messaging, imagery and brand identity are crucial to aid recall. A great example of advertising as a source of brand association is Coca-Cola's Christmas television advertisement. It has become a staple of British viewing to an extent that the consumer looks for it at that time of year. The brand is clear and the message engages emotionally with the viewer.

Case Study – Coca-Cola

With a brand value estimated at $771,839,000, the Coca-Cola brand has been one of the highest valued brands for many years. It continues to receive enormous exposure through top-tier sponsorships with popular events like the FIFA World Cup. Additionally, Coca-Cola ties itself closely with meaningful promotions relating to CSR programmes including disaster relief, youth empowerment and sustainability issues around the globe. This included the wide rollout of its PlantBottle™, a sustainable and recyclable bottle made partially of plant material, which included Heinz adopting the technology for use with ketchup bottles.

The soft drinks market is stable despite the economic climate and this is shown with Coca-Cola's 8% increase in brand value. Their company reports state that consumers worldwide choose to refresh themselves with 1.8 billion Coca-Cola products consumed daily and they have over 50 million fans on Facebook.

PR – is a very important tool for reinforcing and maintaining a brand and, because of its ability to engage and invoke two-way communication, helps to build brand values. The careful placement of articles and the use of opinion leaders and opinion formers are critical to getting across the values of the brand. The unbiased nature of subsequent reporting or opinion pieces gives more credibility to the messages when received by the target audience. In addition organising or sponsoring the right event adds to the 'humanity' of a brand and can be combined with CSR projects to add a strong emotional value. Sponsorship at the corporate level helps increase awareness of the brand and align it with characteristics that the audience will value e.g. car manufacturers and Formula1.

Sales Promotion - although this has traditionally been seen as having a price rather than a value orientation, (Fill has described it as "perceived as a tool that erodes rather than helps build a brand" it can be used strategically (Fill, op.cit.). Sales promotion reinforces the 'value for money' (VFM) aspects of a brand which is particularly important during a recession. For some high quality, high value brands sales promotion is of limited use but it can be used to add to its exclusivity e.g. special shopping events exclusively for loyalty card customers. Others have successfully combined sales promotion techniques with other value added services in order to build brand loyalty. One of the best exponents of this is Tesco.

The digital implication for sales promotion for VFM brands has been the rise of online coupons and 'cashback' sites. For many brands the consequence has been that their products are permanently 'on offer'.

Personal selling – whilst for many products, personal selling has limited brand building capability it is essential when talking about a service. In this case the sales team often *is* the brand.

Direct marketing – direct mail is a very flexible tool and for some organisations is a means of maintaining regular communication with target audiences who have become swamped by electronic media.

Here, the brand values can be personalised and targeted and reinforced in terms of the quality of the photographs, text, and even texture of the mailing. Other tools, such as Direct Response TV (DRTV), are primarily about gaining a sale or response and less about brand reinforcement. However, it must not undermine the brand values in its terminology or placement.

Point of sale merchandising - supports and reinforces all of the above media by representing the characteristics of the brand at the point of purchase e.g. the cosmetics counters in Boots which reinforce the professionalism of the make-up on offer; tasting stands in the supermarket which emphasise local sourcing; and shelf displays of 3 for 2 on crisps – all of which reflect different brand attributes and values.

3.2 Online brands

The internet has changed the way many established brands have had to operate. Lower costs for internet-based organisations and the rise in online purchasing have presented both challenges and opportunities. Online retailers had found a niche and an alternative distribution channel that meant they could offer a cheaper product but with the same quality of both product and service.

There are two levels of branding to consider here: the brand of the product and the brand of the online retailer.

Products with strong established brands have been better placed to move to a multichannel distribution policy and use digital marketing to promote their brands. The problem online marketing brings is differentiation between brands with similar offerings targeted at similar markets. Traditionally the nature of the service encounter was a key tool used to develop brand differentiation for these types of products but with limited customer touch points come limited opportunities to provide a superior delivery of service. The price, transaction process and delivery become crucial to the brand association. Loyalty schemes, customer care lines and relationship marketing help to support the brand.

So, for example, John Lewis with its strong brand has been able to move online very successfully whilst ensuring that its website, online communications, transaction process, delivery and after sales support for online purchases remain true to their brand values.

The second brand issue to consider is that of the online retailer. Through effective brand building in terms of customer service and delivery, organisations like Amazon and Play.com have been able to guarantee quality to a discerning public whilst others in the marketplace have failed even though they were offering the same brands of products.

The point is that both levels of branding have to be right. If you market your products through an online retailer their brand image affects your brand image. If you are marketing a high quality high value brand then selling it through ebay can undermine your brand values. There is a lot of online competition – so who do customers trust.... the trust comes through the brand.

Google and Amazon are just two organisations who have utilised e-commerce and are now hugely successful organisations whose business models are used as case studies around the globe for both innovation and diversification.

A third issue currently taxing the marketer is the need to integrate and harmonise online and offline marketing communications. Again consistency is key and never forget that it is the user experience that counts and users live in the physical world not just on-line!

3.3 Co-branding and partnership marketing

An increasing number of organisations, especially in the B2B sector, have recognised the value of co-branding or partnership marketing opportunities.

For example, a service provider may collaborate with a distributor on marketing campaigns to split costs and leverage the individual strengths of both brands.

Some organisations that operate in similar markets will work together to produce a new product or deliver marketing campaigns.

More intriguing is when two very different brands collaborate on a new product or marketing. One example of this is when Nike and Apple worked together and linked Nike running shoes with Apple's iPods. They leveraged the passion for listening to music when running or exercising, to produce co-branded merchandising of MP3 players. Runners could listen to music and see how far and fast they had run and even how many calories they had used up!

Charities and organisations in the not-for-profit sectors are also increasingly using co-branding with commercial organisations to increase exposure to key stakeholders. For example, the relationship between a charity and a high street retailer can be mutually beneficial in increasing brand awareness and associations. The retailer can use PR and CSR to support their brand values and the charity can increase awareness through a stronger brand and value-added services, and use retail opportunities for fundraising and increasing income.

One of the key benefits of co-branding is that it enables a brand to be introduced to new people who already feel positively towards the partner brand. Small or large organisations can benefit from these types of arrangement. However, the disadvantages should also be noted:

1. The impact is diluted across two brands and the credit and results of a successful campaign may be equally divided – though this is still better than no positive results at all.

2. A negative experience or coverage of one brand may affect the partner brand, whether there was any involvement or not. It is also hard to disassociate from the fact that a brand is relying on its partner's brand equity, which may under some circumstances make a brand look weak or secondary.

Before undertaking a co-branding project, you must ensure that your own guidelines are clearly set and not diverted from. Service Level Agreements are very useful in these circumstances to ensure both parties are clear about the objectives, actions and strategy.

3.4 International branding

Open markets and better integration of global markets has stimulated greater awareness of international marketing opportunities. Marketing communication tools, especially digital, provide cost-effective ways of entering international markets, however, there are challenges that need to be considered:

- There will be cultural differences, which will result in differences in consumer needs, wants, and usage patterns for products and services in comparison to the UK market.
- In certain countries, digital marketing may not be appropriate. Even if it is, there may be differences in consumer response to marketing mix elements.
- Global markets may be more competitive than an organisation's own domestic sector. Competitors based in those markets may have the edge in terms of economies of scale and cost base.
- There may be differences in the legal environment, some of which may conflict with the laws and regulations of the UK market.
- There is a need to take into account language barriers, for example, the meanings of words, symbols, etc. In trying to ensure brand consistency, marketers may find that when translated, a word quite harmless in the UK means something entirely different abroad.
- There may be differences in product placement and administrative procedures.
- Finally, segmentation of the market is further complicated by geography and the global marketing challenges listed above.

All this suggests that organisations need to adopt different strategies for different markets and the conundrum for international marketing communications is whether to standardise or adapt.

A standardised marketing communications strategy across all international markets has the benefit of building global brand recognition and loyalty – which reaps even more benefits as people have become more mobile and more widely travelled.

The alternative is to adapt marketing communications to each local market appealing to local sensibilities, culture and language. This approach is more complicated and costly but may increase brand appeal in different countries. This is an even more appropriate approach if you have adapted you product to the local market.

Chapter 4: Marketing Communications Planning

There are many different approaches to building a Marketing Communications (marcoms) plan. One of the best is PR Smith's SOSTAC® Planning System which provides a consistent template for all plans and a good overview of the issues that need to be addressed (Smith, 2004).

SOSTAC® is an acronym for the six basic elements of a marketing plan:

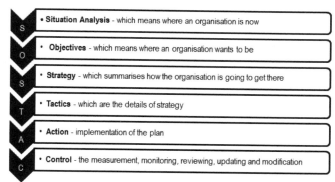

Figure 4.1 Overview of SOSTAC®
Reproduced with kind permission of PR Smith. SOSTAC® is a registered trade mark of PR Smith, www.prsmith.org.

Many marketers often only deal with the SOS of SOSTAC®: a **Situation Analysis** or audit setting out where the organisation is now, setting **Objectives** for where the organisation wants to be, and outlining a **Strategy** for getting there. What they fail to do is develop and implement a detailed, controllable and measurable action plan. The result is that you have no clear perception of how, or if, the objectives have been achieved.

4.1 Situation analysis or audit

It is critical to do a contextual audit of the current situation of the company and the brand prior to setting communications objectives. There is a range of audit tools available including SWOT analysis and PESTER which structure a factually based review of the organisation's internal and external environment: what are the organisation's key strengths, weaknesses, opportunities and threats; what are the factors affecting it?

In addition, no marketing communications activity takes place in a vacuum. There are always other activities and campaigns going on in the customer's environment. We need to take note of these plus the previous impression that our company/brand has left in the market: the success of a new campaign will be impacted by the residual impact of past campaigns.

As with a Marketing Plan we need to conduct an 'Audit of the Environment' including an assessment of:

- The internal **S**trengths and **W**eaknesses of our marketing structure and skills as well as the perceived **O**pportunities and **T**hreats affecting the organisation and in comparison to the competition in the market (SWOT)
- What is happening in the macro PESTER environment i.e. are there any **P**olitical issues; what are the **E**conomic conditions; issues in **S**ociety; new **T**echnologies; **E**nvironmental attitudes; and **R**egulatory contexts that we need to take account of before we set our plan?
- What our competitors are doing - what campaigns, new product development (NPD), etc.
- Stakeholders' understanding and awareness of our brand
- The reach of our marketing communications purchasing power vs. the competition

To conduct a sound audit, and indeed to construct the marcoms plan in general, accurate data is essential.

Market research is discussed in more detail in the Research Handbook but, basically, we need Quantitative data to be able to set out objectives and Qualitative data to construct our brand messages and values. We also need to consider both primary data (new data collected from research we undertake) and secondary data (information which already exists but has been generated by others). Secondary data which already exists should be considered *first*! It may be data that has been generated internally or it may be external data which the internet has made much easier to find. Be careful to remember that, whilst using secondary data may be much cheaper and quicker, it has been collected by someone else for another purpose – make sure it is accurate and relevant.

Quantitative research is "undertaken using a structured research approach with a sample of the population to produce quantifiable insights into behaviour, motivations and attitudes" (Wilson, 2006).

Quantitative research is about asking people for their opinions in a structured way so that measured facts and statistics are collected for comparison. Tools may include face-to-face or online surveys and telephone interviews.

Qualitative research is "research that is undertaken using an unstructured research approach with a small number of carefully selected individuals to produce non-quantifiable insights into behaviour, motivations and attitudes" (Wilson, 2006).

Qualitative research seeks out the 'why', not the 'how' through the analysis of unstructured information. It provides the detail which statistical, quantitative research does not deliver. It gains insight into the attitudes, behaviours, value systems, concerns, motivations, aspirations, culture and lifestyles of the consumer. In terms of marketing communications, tools may include the use of focus groups, in-depth interviews and observation of trial usage. Qualitative research also involves the analysis of any unstructured material, including customer feedback forms, reports or media clips.

4.2 Objectives

When planning any marketing campaign you need to set objectives and targets that can be quantifiably measured so that the campaign can be monitored and controlled. Marcoms objectives should be based on understanding an organisation's strengths, weaknesses and the business environment it is operating in i.e. where you are now, and set out where you want to be or what you want to achieve.

They should also be linked to the organisation's overall business strategy and marketing objectives which flow from the corporate objectives. Corporate objectives are usually financial. For example, they may include "to increase revenue by x% next year". This is interpreted in the Marketing Plan as an objective to increase market share. The marcoms objective would then be to increase the number of customers or the amount each customer spends. The objective for each media can then be defined as an increase in awareness, number of enquiries or amount of cross selling.

All objectives should be SMART. The SMART acronym stands for specific, measurable, achievable, realistic and time bound:

- **Specific** – for example, an organisation might set an objective of getting ten new customers
- **Measurable** – whatever the objective is, it needs to be measurable in some way, either financial or in terms of customer numbers, etc. to check whether targets have been reached
- **Achievable** – the organisation must have the resources required to achieve the objective – the key resources are usually people and money
- **Realistic** – targets should be ambitious but not unachievable because if they are unreasonable they seem out of reach
- **Time-bound** – there should be a deadline for achieving the objective, for example, obtaining ten new customers within the next 12 months

Some examples include:

To grow: The business may set an objective to grow by 15% year on year for the next five years.

Market share: Objectives can be set to achieve a certain level of market share within a specified time, for example, to obtain a 3% market share by 2012.

Advertising: To increase brand awareness by 10% by the end of the year.

Objectives that meet these criteria help marketers to monitor and control a campaign over the course of its duration.

In order to deliver an effective marcoms plan it is also important to establish Creative Objectives for what the impact and reaction should be for each communications tool we use. These will involve variables such as perception, attitudes, knowledge and creating new levels of prompted and spontaneous awareness. Ultimately, communications are designed to meet three objectives:

- **Awareness –** increase brand awareness and establish brand recognition
- **Trial –** stimulate trial purchase
- **Reinforcement –** stimulate and reinforce brand loyalty

4.3 Strategy setting

Again as with Marketing Plans the Marcoms Plan needs to set out how we are going to achieve our objectives: our strategy for getting where we want to be. In doing this we need to define the target markets and the positioning we are going to follow; and we need to define the brand values that we want to promote.

We will look at Brand Strategy in more detail in Chapter 5 but it is worth noting here that in determining strategy it is also important to make sure we encompass more than just the marketing communications media but look at the other elements of the marketing mix as each of these has an impact on our marketing communications strategy:

- **Product** – the value proposition of the offering we make influences customers' perception. So we need to consider issues such as product attributes as well as design and packaging, and the message they give about quality and value.

- **Price** – this is part of positioning the brand. Some customers seek a low price to meet their budgets, while others may view a low price as an indication of poor quality so decisions about price and discounting are crucial.

- **Place** – How and where the product is sold or service is delivered impacts on the image of the brand. Using different distribution channels on the internet or high street retailers says something about your offering.

- **People** – The quality of our people and the service they offer these days is key – it can be the only difference between service brands. So internal marketing to ensure that all employees have the right training and understanding is critical.

- **Processes** – Having the right processes in place will ensure that an organisation offers a consistent service that suits its customer's requirements and delivers on the brand promise that your marcoms promote.

- **Physical evidence** – The appearance of employees and an organisation's premises can affect how customers see the brand. Even the quality of paperwork, such as invoices, makes a difference and needs to reflect the desired brand identity.

4.4 Tactics and implementation

Once the objectives and strategy have been set, the tactics need to be planned including which promotional tools, discussed in Chapter 2 should be utilised. When deciding on tactics a number of factors should be taken into account including: the brand values; target audience; company resources available; and the reach, impact and cost of the media. You should also consider:

Control of the message - in order to match the needs of the target audience and to generate the desired response. Control of the message can be complicated by the use of third-party suppliers or by external events within the market. For example, a communication message can get mangled by a distributor, or an advertisement for a new car may be discredited by a major news story about safety checks or even an accident. Advertising and sales promotion provide the most control over the message, but it is harder to get feedback.

Control of the process - the use of agencies to implement a marcoms campaign can run the risk that the message may get confused and misinterpreted. The best deterrent is to ensure that all agency work is thoroughly checked and approved to prevent the release of inappropriate creative work.

Credibility of the medium – the best tool for this is PR because the target audience will perceive the media as a third party and unbiased towards the organisation. PR has more credibility than advertising, sales promotion and personal selling.

Effectiveness of the medium – the effectiveness of different communication media revolves around the size and geographic scope of the target audience. To communicate to a national audience, tools most suitable for mass communication should be used, for example, advertising and sales promotion. Of course, segmentation and targeting can narrow the scope and increase effectiveness. Mass communication has its limitations, and for specialist businesses sales effort may need personal attention to explain, design, demonstrate, install and service complex equipment.

Most marcoms plans will include a mix of tools and media. The most important thing is to ensure the promotional mix selected reinforces rather than contradicts the brand values. To succeed in achieving goals, marketers must develop communications that:

- Gain attention and engage the consumer
- Communicate a clear message
- Improve general consumer attitude towards a brand
- Reinforce positive attitude towards a brand

4.5 Resources

Smith refers to marketing resource requirements as the 3Ms: Men, Money and Minutes (Smith, op. cit):

Men (Human Resource) – all of the skills and expertise needed for the different elements of a campaign may not exist within the marketing function. These include:

- **Creative Skills** - copywriting, design, and audio and visual flair to create the campaign
- **Diagnostic skills** – to analyse the reason for failing marketing campaigns
- **Implementation skills** – marketers need to be able to manage teams, allocate resources, organise, manage budgets and motivate colleagues and employees to complete tasks
- **Evaluation skills** – to monitor and evaluate marketing actions

Some organisations may need to outsource work as a result. In addition the company may not have the equipment and software needed to create the campaign. Does it have the picture and logo files, the fonts and correct text files? N.B. most companies run PC systems; most agencies and printers run Mac!

Money – Section 4.6 will discuss budgeting in more detail, however, it is important that the expenditure is relevant to the objectives and the scale of the organisation.

A marketer must ask the question, have we got the money to achieve this? If not, then adjust the objectives. If the objectives are measurable then return on investment can be calculated.

Minutes – Timing is important! For example, if a new product is being released, different marketing communications may be scheduled before, during and after the release date. This has already been discussed in terms of the product lifecycle. Marketers must ensure that there are clear timescales, schedules and deadlines to ensure there is enough time and that the correct messages are communicated at the right time.

These elements are crucial when considering a campaign. When developing objectives, strategy and tactics, a marketer must ensure these are in line with the appropriate resources available.

4.6 Budgeting
A budget is a consolidated statement of the resources required to achieve objectives or to implement planned activities. It is a tool for planning and controlling a project's expenditure. It controls by having a plan against which actual results can be continually compared.

When setting a budget for a marketing communications campaign, it is essential to ensure that the budget is relevant to the objectives set. If a sales target has been set then the budget needs to be set at a level, where income will be higher than the expenditure allocated. Cost Benefit Analysis (CBA) is a useful tool to help marketers to set budgets and ensure that a return on investment is taken into account. In CBA all of the costs and all of the benefits (both in monetary terms) are calculated over time.

These can then be used to calculate the payback period, average or internal rate of return on the investment and the 'net present value' (NPV) i.e. the value of the costs and benefits over time discounted back to give a current value.

Other models that are used for setting budgets for communication campaigns are:

- **Marginal analysis -** this is the examination of the additional benefits of a campaign compared to its additional costs. Organisations use marginal analysis to help maximise profits.
- **Affordable -** this is as it sounds: spending what is affordable. This is not based on any research into the cost of a campaign but is set on the basis that promotion is viewed as essential and designed around the amount felt necessary to maintain a certain brand presence. The budget is allocated from company surpluses.
- **Objective and task -** this is where an organisation allocates its budget based on the objectives of the campaign. Allocation is based on the tasks required and the costs associated with those tasks. This method is quantified and can be monitored quite simply.
- **Percentage of sales -** the percentage-of-sales method allocates the marcoms budget based on forecast sales or current sales. Allocation is based on the revenue so when revenue goes up, the budget goes up and vice versa.
- **Competitive parity -** this is when an organisation tries to match its budget to competitors. This may be to try to emulate the success of a competitor's campaign. However, this can have its problems; for example, a competitor may have a lower cost base allowing more funds to be available to marketing activity.
- **The investment model** – this is sometimes used by organisations where the promotional budget is set according to the amount felt necessary to maintain a certain brand value.

Chapter 5: Developing a Brand Strategy

As we have seen in Chapter 4, determining the right brand strategy is a crucial part of the marketing communications planning process. There is a wide variety of strategies that might be adopted and they are not mutually exclusive. The following are some of the key options which should be considered and if appropriate adopted and adapted.

5.1 Line extension

Brand line extension is when a company introduces a new item in the same product range using an established product's brand name. For example, Diet Coke is a line extension of the parent brand Coke. While the products have distinct differences, they are in the same product category and the extension (Diet Coke) is very dependent initially on customer recognition of the brand name Coke.

According to Giddens and Hofmann: "More than half of all new products introduced each year are brand line extensions. New flavours, package sizes, nutritional content or products containing special additives are included in this definition" (Giddens and Hofmann, 2011).

The benefits of line extension include:

- Expanding company shelf space presence
- Gaining more potential customers
- Offering customers more variety
- Greater marketing efficiency
- Greater production efficiency
- Lower promotional costs
- Increased profits

Brand line extensions reduce the risk associated with new product development due to the established success of the parent brand. The consumers buying decision is already influenced by the trust they have with the established brand. As a result, promotional costs are much lower because there is not so much need for exposure and awareness building.

Additionally, more products expand a company's shelf space presence enhancing brand recognition. For example, Kellogg's will have the largest share of shelf space in the cereals section as it increases its line of products, and this is replicated across all supermarkets as the main competition is own-brand labels that will differ from store to store.

There are threats to this strategy including the damage to an established brand if the new product is faulty, does not sell well or conversely its success initiates possible intra-firm competition.

5.2 Brand extension

Brand extension is when an organisation does not just re-enter an existing market place with a new product; it enters a new category. e.g. cosmetics brands moving into shampoo.

Before an organisation extends a brand into a new product or service category, they must be clear about what the original brand stands for, what people associate it with and what its personality is. Then the question is will these qualities be beneficial to marketing in the new category. They also need to consider what the effect will be on the existing brand. Ideally, it will enhance its perception and broaden its appeal, not damage or reduce it.

VanAuken has identified some examples of **un**successful brand extensions (VanAuken, 2011):

- **Levi's classic tailored suits** - What do people most often associate with Levi's and how does that relate to suits?
- **Bayer 'Aspirin-Free'** - What is Bayer most often associated with and how does that relate to 'aspirin-free'? If Bayer feels the need to offer an 'aspirin-free' product, what does that say about their core products?
- **Bic perfume in your pocket** - Because Bic is associated with small, less expensive, disposable things that fit in your pocket, what is wrong with this thinking?

5.3 Corporate branding

Corporate branding is more than the company logo, design style and colour scheme. Although these are important elements they are just part of a corporate brand. Corporate branding should encompass the vision and values of an organisation, its leadership and management style, its culture and its image in the eyes of its stakeholders.

A strong corporate branding strategy can add significant value in terms of helping the entire corporation and the management team to implement the long-term vision, create unique positions in the market place for the company and its offering, and not least to unlock the leadership potential within the organisation. A corporate branding strategy can enable the corporation to leverage its tangible and non-tangible assets.

A great example of successful corporate branding is HSBC Bank. In recent years it has acquired a vast number of companies globally and adapted them to its international corporate brand with great success. HSBC epitomises how a strong corporate brand builds and maintains strong perceptions in the minds of its customers.

5.4 Generic

Porter's famous Generic Strategies, although originally applied at the corporate level, can also be useful at brand level (Porter, 1985). His analysis suggests that some of the most basic choices faced by companies are the choice of markets that the company should serve and how the company should compete in those selected markets. He then identified three generic strategies for organisations to achieve competitive advantage: cost leadership, differentiation, and focus. The same approach can be taken when thinking about strategies for brands.

Cost leadership – companies attempt to become the lowest-cost producers in a market segment. The company with the lowest costs will earn the highest profits when the competing products are essentially undifferentiated e.g. Amazon at corporate level and Tesco Value at product level.

Differentiation – when a company differentiates its products, it is often able to charge a premium price for its products or services in the market. Some general examples of differentiation include better service levels to customers, better product performance, etc. in comparison with existing competitors e.g. Apple at corporate level and Lexus at product level.

Focus – this is often identified as a moderator of the two other generic strategies. Companies employ this strategy by focusing on areas in a market where there is a defendable niche often with the least amount of competition. This strategy gives an organisation the option of charging a premium price for superior quality (differentiation focus) or of offering a low price product to a small and specialised group of buyers (cost focus) e.g. Hotel Chocolate at corporate level and Naxos at product level (cheap classical music CDs).

According to Porter, a company's failure to make a choice between these generic strategies essentially implies that the company is stuck in the middle with no competitive advantage (Porter, 1980). At brand level this might mean it has no brand personality or perceived brand value.

5.5 Own-label

The concept of own-label brands is quite simple and has been around for over 100 years. The manufacturer (who has a limited end user relationship) produces goods or services for the retailer who has an intense customer relationship and thereby a strong ability to create brand loyalty. This plays to the strengths of both parties. Some branded manufacturers also undertake 'own work' in order to gain greater market share even though the own-label will compete against their own brand.

The leading UK and American supermarkets have expanded their own-label product ranges to the extent of offering a range from high quality to value-brands and a diverse range of sub-brands from premium food to clothing. One of the most famous own-label brands to have emerged from the UK supermarket chains is Asda's George clothing range.

This is estimated to be worth around £1.2bn in annual sales – making Asda one of the leading clothing retailers in the UK (Goldfingle and Lawson, 2013).

Sales of own-label food products in the UK now represent over 20% of total UK food sales. These own-label supermarket products have now become brands in their own right with their own customer loyalty.

The success of these supermarket brands has led to many other retailers entering the market (e.g. John Lewis) and this is not confined to products. Many insurance services are often white labelled versions of major brands.

5.6 Multi-branding

With multiple products or services a company needs to decide how it is to brand its range. There are different approaches:

A family brand – such as Heinz. The advantages are only having one brand image and set of values to manage and promote, and the high recognition and loyalty that can be generated. New product introduction is simpler. The downside is that one product error or failing can damage the entire image.

Individual product brands – such as Proctor & Gamble's Fairy, Ariel & Daz (visit www.pg.com to see the huge range of brands they own). This approach has a number of advantages. By adopting a multi-brand strategy, an organisation can obtain greater space in the market and leave less space for the competition. In addition, by promoting similar products under different brand names, an organisation can fill any gaps in the market, thereby, saturating it. In every market, there are some customers who frequently change brands in order to experiment. This strategy counters this threat. The obvious downside with the strategy is cannibalisation of sales by your own products.

Another good example of multi-branding is Unilever. Unilever has to manage brands across different markets from Food to Beauty to Nutrition to Health. They are similar markets but each brand has gained market share on its own strengths. In fact 150 million times a day, someone, somewhere chooses a Unilever product like Ben & Jerry's, Carte D'Or, Dove, Lynx, Persil, Cif, etc. These all have their own brand identities, values and levels of customer awareness. However, Unilever has started to take a different approach and promote its parent company name alongside its product brands in order to build its corporate brand as well as its product brands.

5.7 Push, pull and profile strategies

Push, Pull and Profile describe three different approaches to marketing communications strategies. It is not necessary to choose just one approach. It may be relevant to have a balance between Push, Pull and Profile depending on the product, the type of market and the structure of the organisation's channel management.

Push strategies

A Push strategy is when an organisation promotes a service or product to retailers and distributors in order to encourage them to 'push' or promote the product to the end-user. The main aim is to get the product into the hands of the consumer with little to no advertising effort.

This strategy usually requires personal selling and field marketing to acquire a customer. For example, trade shows are a good way of implementing a Push marketing strategy as there are plenty of opportunities to speak to people with a vested interest. A Push strategy makes use of an organisation's sales force to create demand. The producer promotes the product to distributors, the distributor promotes it to retailers, and the retailers promote it to consumers.

Push strategies work well where:

- there is low brand loyalty;
- many acceptable substitutes are available in the market;
- relatively new products are to be launched;

- the product purchase is unplanned or on impulse; and
- the consumer is familiar and has reasonably adequate knowledge about the product

Push strategy

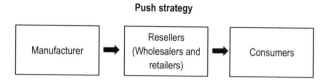

Figure 5.1 Push strategy

Pull strategies

A Pull strategy involves communicating directly with the end customer or consumer to attract them (or 'pull' them) to the retailer and distributor in order to purchase the product. Costs tend to be higher for a Pull strategy because it usually entails a mix of advertising and sales promotion to a mass market. This spend is required to raise awareness and stimulate demand for a product or service.

Pull strategies work well where:

- it is possible to differentiate the product on the basis of real or emotional features;
- brand consumers show a high degree of involvement in the product purchase;
- there is reasonably high brand loyalty; and
- consumers make the brand choice decision before they go to the store.

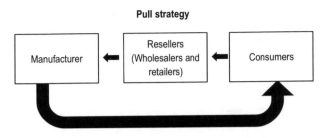

Figure 5.2 Pull strategy

Profile strategies

A Profile strategy is used to satisfy an organisation's corporate promotional goals in order to satisfy stakeholders' requirements. The primary objective of a Profile strategy is to build awareness, perception, attitudes and reputation. This might be through promotional tools such as PR, sponsorship or corporate advertising.

Digital marketing – pull versus push

Push and Pull strategies can also be used in digital marketing.

Pull digital marketing entails activity in which the consumer must actively seek the marketing content. This could be via web searches, websites, blogs and streaming media (audio and video). In this context, each user has to link to the website to view the content. Additional internet marketing technologies, for example search engine optimisation, may be required to attract the desired consumer demographic.

Push digital marketing entails activity where the marketer sends the content to the consumer, for example, emails, text messaging and web feeds (in which the marketer sends the messages to subscribers). Push technologies can deliver content immediately it becomes available and is better targeted to its consumer demographic, although audiences are often smaller and the cost for creation and distribution is higher.

Chapter 6: Evaluation
6.1 Purpose of evaluation

Evaluation of marketing communication tools, the media used and campaigns executed is an essential part of any marketing communications. You will recall that in Chapter 4 we looked at SOSTAC® where the 'C' stands for control: measurement, monitoring, reviewing, updating and modification. It is only by evaluating its activities that an organisation can learn and improve.

The aim is to assess both whether the communications have been effective and been undertaken efficiently. Lessons learned can be fedback into the next planned communications, successes built on and disappointments addressed.

There are numerous methods or 'analytics' (both formal and informal) for evaluation and it is not possible to consider all of them in this Handbook. However, we will look at some overarching principles, good practice and examples. More detail on the tools and techniques can be found in the Research and Digital handbooks.

It should also be said at the outset that evaluating the effectiveness of marcoms is notoriously difficult. You will be familiar with the quote variously attributed to William Lever and John Wanamaker: "Half the money I spend on advertising is wasted; the trouble is I don't know which half."

Consumers do not always respond to a communication quickly; sometimes they do not always realise that a purchase made was initially prompted by a communication received some time ago, neither do they always conveniently respond in the way expected (perhaps responding to an email campaign with a letter or text) and, of course, they forget. They do not always remember all the media they have seen or even the most recent media seen before making a purchase. But this does not mean we should not evaluate as much as possible!

6.2 Principles of good practice

There are a number of overarching principles of good practice that are useful to bear in mind for any marcoms evaluation:

1. Build in your intention to evaluate right at the beginning of your communication or campaign. Be clear about what you want to achieve and identify how you are going to measure that achievement. Remember, the importance of setting those SMART objectives! The most important thing is to assess the success in achieving the promotional objectives set in the first place.

2. Select evaluation tools that are appropriate for the communication tools used and the objectives set (see Section 6.3 below).

3. Put in place baseline data and build in measurement mechanisms as part of your planning process. For example, if your objective is to increase interest in your product (SMART objective: to generate 500 additional enquiries in the next 6 months) you need to establish the number of enquiries you have had in the last 6 months (or an average over a longer period) and ensure that the enquiry response mechanism clearly links the response to the campaign (a code on a coupon or reference to quote to be eligible for an offer).

4. Pre-test as well as post-test. Pre-testing a communication can help you improve its effectiveness as part of its development (e.g. pre-testing advertisements or a range of sales promotion offers to assess impact and reaction). Pre-testing can include: concept testing, focus groups, consumer juries and physiological tests. You can also use pre-testing to establish baseline information such as levels of awareness, corporate or brand image held.

5. Establish a Customer Panel which you can survey regularly and use for pre- and post-testing. This is especially valuable for organisations which have limited direct contact with their customers.

6. There should be a balance between qualitative and quantitative methods of evaluation. The early use of quantitative methods during planning, (A/B testing) results in directly measurable and comparable outcomes that can be evaluated at the end of the campaign. Qualitative evaluation of awareness and attitudes is much more subjective in comparison but if sourced both pre- and post-implementation, this data can still be compared. Fill says: "the balance in testing advertising is to use a greater proportion of qualitative than quantitative methods. The balance with sales promotions is shifted the other way" (Fill, 2006).

7. Establish good practice internally – whenever possible, ensure staff who have contact with enquirers or purchasers ask how they heard about the company/product/offer and keep a record and feedback this information. Whenever possible automate. Track your sales, enquiries, responses, etc.

8. Monitor progress during the promotion or campaign: both costs and benefits. Do not just wait to see what has happened when it has finished especially if it runs for a length of time. Remember the SWOT and PESTER analysis undertaken – keep an eye on those weaknesses and threats.

6.3 Evaluation tools

As we have already said the method(s) of evaluation selected need to be appropriate for the promotional tool used and the objectives set. The Research Handbook looks at these tools in more depth. Let's consider some examples:

Advertising – objectives may be to increase sales but also to increase awareness or knowledge or to change perceptions about a brand or organisation. For these you need to use pre- and post-testing to measure recall, understanding and opinions.

Surveys, focus groups, consumer panels, recall, recognition and sales tests are all useful tools and will provide quantitative and qualitative data such as the number of people who recall the advert or recognise the brand, or their perception of the organisation or brand. Remember that advertising may also be seeking to achieve changes over a longer period of time than say sales promotion. Objectives may be both communications and behavioural-related changes, under these circumstances both should be measured.

PR – objectives may be to increase awareness of the organisation, change perceptions of the organisation or brand, or limit the damage of a crisis! Measurement can be both quantitative and qualitative. You can measure outputs such as the number of column inches or pieces of coverage a story attained, the number of publications carrying the story, broadcast time of company stories, exposure (gained by adding up readership, viewer or listener figures) and the cost of comparative coverage through advertising.

It is more difficult to measure the impact of PR in terms of an organisation's reputation. One way that this can be achieved is through perception surveys and benchmarking awareness amongst stakeholders. Repeating the research before, during and after a campaign will provide analysis data on the perception of a brand, service or organisation.

Sales promotion – objectives are usually related to increasing sales or trials or even the number of coupons returned and have a shorter time frame than advertising. Quantitative data can be collected in terms of the number of coupons returned, entries to a competition, items sold (using the retailer's electronic point of sale (EPOS) system). It is also worth bearing in mind that by undertaking longer term tracking of sales you can assess the impact of sales promotions.

Personal selling – sales staff should have clear targets set as SMART objectives in their job description or contract. Sales made need to be monitored and reviewed against the target(s).

Bear in mind that evaluation needs to include measurement of the effort put in as well as the sales achieved. So to measure performance fully you may need to also measure the size of sales, the number of calls or visits made, or the number of new accounts secured as opposed to repeat sales.

Direct Marketing – targets are set for response levels for each media used and the responses received through each media can be recorded. Bear in mind though that consumers may respond through a different medium! Tools include putting a reference to quote or code on a coupon or mailing so that a response can be traced back to the specific communication. Objectives are more likely to include behavioural change - it may not be a purchase or making an enquiry but visiting a store or website. Whatever specific objective is set make sure you also put in place mechanisms for measuring the behaviour you are targeting.

Point of Sale – objectives are likely to be related to numbers sampling or buying a product. You can count sampling or purchases by the amount consumed or through EPOS.

Digital – objectives for digital communications are likely to encompass all aspects from increased sales to response/ behavioural change to changes in attitudes and perceptions. Measuring the results of digital communications in terms of outputs, sales, responses, etc. can be easier than for traditional methods.

For example, replies to emails, downloads, clicks on a website, clicks on PPC adverts, click-through rates, usage, time spent on a page, bounce rates, etc. can all be measured. Marketing dashboards, such as Google Analytics, provide information on the source of a click through all the way down to tracking data for a user's journey around the site. Visit: www.google.com/analytics for more information.

Social Media – at present the jury is still out on how to measure social media but most organisations use the simple and readily available measures of numbers of followers, 'likes' and shares based on the premise that the greater the awareness of the organisation or a product the more this will stimulate word of mouth.

Responses to posts and comments on blogs are also a good measure of success but, of course, these need to be looked at in terms of whether they are positive, neutral or negative.

Part 2: Buyer Behaviour

Chapter 7: Buyer Behaviour

This part of the Handbook looks at buyer behaviour in both a B2B and B2C context.

7.1 Buyer, consumer, customer – what are the differences?

The use of the term consumer and customer are commonly interchanged but in reality mean different things. A consumer is the ultimate end-user of a product or service. A customer is not always the end-user. For example, they may be purchasing for resale. It is important to distinguish this difference, and the target audience, accordingly when looking at behaviour.

7.2 Why do we need to understand buyer behaviour?

The simple answer is the need to make our offering and our marketing communications more effective. It is buyer behaviour that dictates buying decisions. We have already discussed why organisations need to communicate with the consumer and the ways in which this can be achieved through the promotional mix. But in order for this to be effective, marketers need to understand how customers and consumers behave. Without this understanding, much of our promotional effort and resource is likely to be wasted.

As part of the planning process, consumer behaviour needs to be understood and reviewed to ensure the correct mix of communications and the right media are selected. The current economic environment adds to the importance of selecting the right media to ensure that marketing delivers value to the organisation.

In addition the significant growth in available communication channels in recent years, and the increasing ability of consumers of all ages to interact with them, means that marketers need to be more creative than ever in communicating with their target audience

IT has enabled consumers from a wide variety of backgrounds to interact with organisations in different ways.

This can be clearly seen with the huge growth in the use of social media platforms such as Facebook, LinkedIn and Twitter. As a result, understanding consumer behaviour has never been more vital.

7.3 The importance of 'customers'

The modern customer, whether in a business, industrial, not-for-profit or consumer market is very sophisticated. Customers are more aware of their power within a given market than ever before. They have specific requirements in terms of needs, wants and desires. As marketers we need to anticipate, identify and meet these requirements in line with the capabilities of our organisation.

Market orientation is how an organisation can achieve a culture where beating the competition through the creation of superior customer value is the paramount objective throughout the business. Understanding customers and their requirements is core to being market oriented.

The customer's perception of value will be linked to many factors including what they will receive and how much it will cost to get it (this is not just about money - it may relate to time, effort and resource, etc.) These perceptions will be different depending on which market sector an organisation is in and who the customer actually is. For example:

- **Services -** in services marketing, including professional services, customer services, medical services, entertainment services, personal care services and maintenance services, the customer will assess the value in terms of the quality of delivery. That may include price, convenience, professionalism of personnel, efficiency, etc. The 3 Ps: People, Process and Physical evidence are key. And the customer is a 'client'.
- **Not-for-profit –** with organisations such as charities, voluntary bodies, cultural institutions and societies a key issue is who their customers are. They do not naturally fall within the earlier definition of a 'customer'. Their target markets are more likely to be donors, sponsors and volunteers, and their 'customers'' perception of value will lie in their affiliation to the cause, the image and reputation of the body.

- **Public sector -** by definition, customers of organisations in this sector are the general 'public'. Examples of public sector organisations include local government, councils, educational establishments, emergency services, etc. Sometimes these organisations are not looking to sell a product or service, but to change behaviour such as 'stop smoking', promote exercise for health or encourage take up of a service. This is known as 'social marketing'.

- **Business to Business (B2B) –** in this sector customers are other businesses. Higher value is likely to be placed on the physical attributes of a product or efficiency of a service rather than on emotional attributes. B2B buying decisions are also subject to different influences and we will look at the difference between B2B and B2C decision making in Sections 7.4 and 7.5. However, it is important to remember that business customers are people too and subject to some of the same influences and behaviours as B2C customers.

- **Business to Consumer (B2C) –** we are all customers for consumer goods and our own behaviours can provide useful, albeit indicative, insight for our marketing decisions. In earlier times, marketers understood consumers through the daily experience of selling to them. The growth in the size of organisations and markets has removed many marketing decision makers from direct contact with their customers. Increasingly, marketers have had to turn to market and consumer research to obtain the answers to the most important questions about their market.

7.4 Consumer buying behaviour

In terms of marketing communications, what we want to know is how consumers respond to the promotional tools and messages we use. If we are to get the response we want, we need to understand what influences consumers' decisions, what roles they play in a purchase decision and what decision making processes they use.

Influences

Consumers are affected by a wide range of influences outside the control of the marketer. These include cultural and social influences such as peer group pressure and family; and environmental factors such as the economy and technology. We also have to consider individual psychology – including factors such as personality, motivation and learning. Figure 7.1 illustrates the range of influences including the Marketing Mix which impact on consumers' decision making process. We will return to the individual influences in Chapter 8.

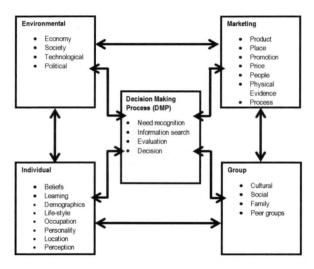

Figure 7.1 Consumer decision making process and influences

Roles

It is also important to recognise that the purchase of many products or services (in B2C as well as B2B) is not always an individual decision. In certain cases, it can involve a Decision Making Unit (DMU) consisting of more than one person.

There are six roles that people might play in a buying decision:

- **Initiator** – the person who first suggests the idea of buying a product or service.
- **Influencer** – a person whose views or advice carry some weight in making the final decision. For example, this could be a family member, a friend or a colleague.
- **Decision-maker** – the person who decides on the major components of any buying decision: whether to buy, what to buy, how to buy, or where to buy.
- **Purchaser** – the person who makes the purchase.
- **User** – the person who actually uses the product or service. Depending on the circumstances of the purchase, this may or may not be the Initiator.
- **Gate-keeper** – these are people who control access to key members of the DMU.

The decision-making process

Buyers go through a number of stages when making a purchase.

- **Need identification** – the buyer recognises a problem or need. This can be triggered by an external stimuli.
- **Information search** – an interested customer searches for more information about different ways to meet their need.
- **Evaluation of alternatives** – most current models of the customer evaluation process are cognitively oriented - that is, they see the consumer as forming product judgments largely on a conscious and rational basis. Factors that are usually weighed up include the benefits and attributes of the product, how important they are to that consumer, and the image they have of the brand or organisation.
- **Purchase decision** – in the evaluation stage, the consumer forms preferences from the choice available. The consumer who decides to purchase will make up to five purchase sub-decisions including:

- o A brand decision
- o A vendor decision
- o A quantity decision
- o A timing decision
- o A payment method decision

- **Post-purchase evaluation** – the process does not end at purchase. After purchasing a product, or experiencing a service, the consumer will experience some level of satisfaction or dissatisfaction. This will not only have a major effect on their likelihood to repurchase but through word of mouth and recommendation may affect the purchase decision of other consumers too. They may be part of another Decision Making Unit!

There are two additional theories on consumer decision making, that also need to be considered. The first relates to the decision making process for new products. The consumer again goes through a series of stages: awareness, interest, evaluation, trial and adoption. However, there is an additional factor to take into account – some people love trying new products; others are less ready to try new things and prefer to wait. Consumers can be classified into 5 different groups according to their readiness to try new things. Figure 7.2 below illustrates the groups, their relative size and the time they are likely to take to adopt an innovation.

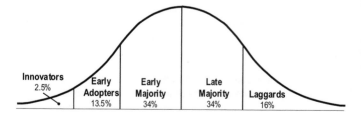

Figure 7.2 Adoption of innovation

For marketers the challenge is to move consumers through the stages from awareness to adoption whilst recognising that customers will make decisions and respond to communications in different ways depending on their willingness to adopt innovation. So for a new product the most effective communications may need to be targeted first at innovators and early adopters but change over time to target the late majority.

The final model is the FCB (Foote, Cone, Belding) Matrix developed by Vaughn (Vaughn, 1980). As Figure 7.3 shows this suggests that customers make decisions and respond to different prompts in different ways depending on their level of involvement with a product or service and whether 'thinking or logic' or 'feeling or emotion' predominate.

	Thinking (logic predominates)	Feeling (emotion predominates)
High Involvement	Informative (learn/feel/do)	Affective (feel/learn/do)
Low Involvement	Habit formation (do/learn/feel)	Self-satisfaction (do/feel/learn)

Figure 7.3 The FCB Matrix (Vaughn, 1980)

Vaughn proposed that by combining involvement with elements of thinking and feeling, four primary advertising planning strategies can be distinguished; these are informative, affective, habitual and self-satisfaction. The four quadrants of the grid identify particular types of decision-making and each requires different communication approaches.

In addition by recognising the different ways in which the decision making process is ordered in each quadrant, he proposed that the 'learn–feel–do' decision making sequence should be visualised as a continuum or circular concept. Communication strategy should, therefore, be based on the point of entry that consumers make to the cycle.

Depending on the quadrant different media and messages will be more effective. In addition some offerings, generally regarded as 'habitual', may be moved to another quadrant, such as 'responsive', to develop differentiation and establish a new position for the product in the minds of consumers relative to the competition.

Figure 7.4 The effectiveness of promotional tools

7.5 Organisational buying behaviour

In B2B marketing and, to a lesser extent service and not-for-profit too, a customer is purchasing a product or service on behalf of another organisation. Marketers need to take into account several considerations not normally found in consumer marketing:

- Organisations buy goods and services to satisfy different goals: making profits, reducing costs, meeting employees' needs, and satisfying legal obligations.
- More people typically participate in organisational buying decisions than in consumer buying decisions, especially in procuring major items. Decision participants usually have different organisational responsibilities and apply different criteria to the purchase decision.
- The buyers must adhere to purchasing policies, constraints and requirements set by their organisations.
- Buying processes often include requests for quotations, proposals and purchase orders - another dimension not typically found in consumer buying.

- The demand for industrial goods can be derived from the demand for consumer goods.
- Organisational markets comprise fewer buyers and are more often concentrated. For example, consider markets such as the food industry – there are very few poultry processing companies in the UK. In addition, buyers may be concentrated geographically, for example, the number of IT companies based on the M4 corridor in the UK.

In general, organisational or business purchases are usually more professional (there may be professionally qualified buyers), more structured and involve more people in the decision making process. They are also usually less 'emotional' and more 'rational', - although, as we have already noted, organisational buyers are still people and so it is important to take into account some of the same influences that affect consumer buying behaviour. A point to note is that the close relationship between buyer and seller in B2B means that personal selling and relationship marketing are important in B2B markets.

Influences
As with consumer buying behaviour, people have their own motivations, perceptions and preferences when purchasing. In a B2B environment these may also be affected by professional status and their attitude towards risk. In addition organisational factors (objectives, procedures and systems); and group or interpersonal factors such as authority, empathy and persuasiveness impact on decisions.

Roles
In organisational buying there may be a larger number of people involved in a purchase decision – especially if it is a high cost, high risk, infrequent purchase.

The DMU, in this instance, includes everyone who plays the following roles:

- **Users** – these are the people who will actually use the end product, for example operators who use production machinery. They may trigger the purchasing process through reporting a need, and may also be consulted on the specifications for whatever is to be bought.
- **Influencers** –provide information which helps with the specification and evaluation. Their expertise may give them the power of veto on a decision. For example, with a PC purchase the IT department will be influential as they have to maintain the PC after purchase.
- **Deciders** – have authority to make a decision. Some organisational structures may dictate the final decision rests with top management. These are the 'Approvers'.
- **Purchasers** – have the authority to select and negotiate with suppliers. Buyers could have different levels of seniority to handle different types of transaction. These individuals do not necessarily belong to a formal purchasing department but are in many cases within a functional role, for example, finance.
- **Gatekeepers** – control the flow of information by denying access to key members of the decision unit. For example purchasing agents or personal secretaries may block access to a decider or approver.

Of course, the roles within the DMU may be taken by a number of individuals or sometimes just one person plays all of the roles, dependent on the structure and size of an organisation. In addition the unit and roles may change for different purchases.

The decision-making process

The decision making process in organisations has similarities with the consumer process:

- **Problem recognition** – the process begins when someone in an organisation identifies a problem or need that can be met by acquiring a product or a service.
  This can occur as a result of internal or external stimuli such as a PC crashing or seeing an advertisement or new product at an exhibition.
- **Need specification** – sets out the details of the requirement and may involve consultation with technical staff.
- **Supplier search and selection** – the DMU will look to identify the most appropriate vendors of the product or service. The more complex and expensive the item, the greater the amount of time they will spend in searching for and evaluating suppliers. Suppliers are then invited to submit proposals, or in some organisations tender for contract. For complex or expensive purchases detailed written proposals will be requested from each potential supplier. The buyer will review the proposals and move towards selection. Assessment will be against a list of key criteria.
- **Decision** – the preferred supplier is selected and the specifics of the order are set out including quantity and warranties.
- **Performance review** – the buyer evaluates the performance of the particular supplier(s) and will make future decisions on repurchase or continued service based on the review.

In summary whether you are marketing B2C or B2B it is essential to understand the influences, roles and processes that your customer goes through in order to select the most effective communications tools and messages.

Chapter 8: Influences and Learning

In Chapter 7 we looked at the range of influences which can have an effect on consumer and organisational buying behaviour. Individual influences such as attitudes and perception play a role in all buying behaviour and these psychological factors influence how people behave, make decisions and respond to stimuli. Understanding these influences and the different ways in which people learn helps inform decisions about your communications campaign, and how to make your messages and choice of media more effective.

8.1 Attitudes and beliefs

Attitudes impinge on virtually everything we do. As part of our everyday lives, we are continually evaluating events and people. Most of our daily activity is directed towards creating a favourable attitude in other people towards ourselves, convincing others that they ought to change their attitude, or justifying our attitude to another person.

Attitudes have been defined as a tendency to respond in a certain way to persons, objects or situations. Our beliefs shape our attitudes and our attitudes determine what we are willing to believe. It is a constantly evolving process.

This is important for marketing communications because beliefs influence the perception of a product or organisation held by a customer, and if some of the beliefs are wrong you will want to change them. Attitudes are hard to change and it is easier to fit your products and messages in with existing attitudes. However, it can be worth trying and much social marketing is aimed at precisely this - think about the '5 a day' campaign.

8.2 Perception

Perception is how people 'see' things. It is a process by which people select and interpret stimuli and form a meaningful picture; a process of comparison, setting incoming information against a background of social experience and psychological disposition - a frame of reference. It is essentially a process of making 'wholes' from parts.

Perceptions about any given situation will be individualised and personalised - two people in the same situation or meeting the same person may have a completely different perception about the event. This is because we all take in, store and make sense of information in a different way.

There are also three other factors at work. People are selective in what they notice, how they interpret the information and in what they remember, and their perceptions vary accordingly. These are known as 'selective attention', 'selective distortion' and 'selective retention'. People by and large believe what they want to believe and pick out what they consider important. Perception has been described as being "more real than reality" and how a customer perceives something *is* their reality.

This provides a key lesson for marketing communications. It is said that people are exposed to between 500 and 5,000 advertisements every day – depending on which side of the Atlantic you live! When that much information is around, people can only pay attention to some of it – they need to filter. Consequently, building attention grabbing, innovative, features into communications can pay dividends. Attention can be caught by:

- Intensity and size
- Position
- Contrast
- Novelty
- Repetition
- Movement

Finally, our perceptions are based on past experiences and pre-conditioning. This explains why there is a heightened awareness of advertising for items individuals are already considering.

8.3 Motivation

Once the individual has the belief and the perception that a product or service is right for them, what is it that motivates them to act on this information?

Humans are said to be 'purposive', which means that there are reasons (motives) for what we do. We all have needs and it is when these needs become strong enough that they motivate us to take action.

One of the main theories of motivation is Maslow's Hierarchy of Needs as shown in Figure 8.1 below.

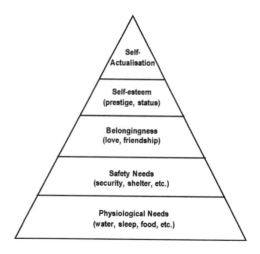

Figure 8.1 Maslow's hierarchy of needs (Maslow, 1943)

Abraham Maslow was a clinical psychologist working on the theory of frustration and neuroses. His work was republished by Douglas McGregor who many will recognise for his Theory X and Theory Y management styles.

The Hierarchy of Needs model assumes that there are many layers to motivation containing both physiological and psychological elements. People need to satisfy their most basic needs (hunger, thirst) but when these have been met they stop being a motivator and people move on to try and satisfy the next level. Self-fulfilment (actualisation) is seen as the highest level of motivation. This suggests that understanding your customers' needs helps to understand what motivates them and enables marketing communications to be positioned more effectively.

Be careful with the hierarchy concept, though. It is not the same in all cultures and does not fully reflect the fact that most of us are trying to satisfy several different needs all at the same time!

8.4 Personality

Personality comprises the unique psychological traits of an individual such as: optimism, confidence, shyness, humour, etc. It is easy to see where individuals' personalities might influence their purchasing behaviour but harder to see how marketers can factor this in to mass communications when everyone is different.

In fact there are several useful concepts here. First, it is often possible to identify a key personality trait that a particular market has in common. An obvious example is that people who like mountain bikes like excitement and action. Marketing communications can build this into their message.

Secondly, if you know something about the types of personality your target customers have you can attribute relevant traits to your brand – i.e. create a brand personality that will appeal to your target market. Examples include Apple and innovation; Innocent and fun.

Finally, there is the concept of self-image – how someone sees themselves (or, perhaps wants to be seen). This recognises that people buy things which contribute to and reflect their self-image. Marketing communications which promote a brand image that meets the self-image shared by a target market are more likely to be successful.

8.5 Groups

Another factor considered in looking at influences on buyer behaviour (and indeed for segmentation) is groups. People belong to groups such as family and professional associations, and also have 'reference' groups which influence their behaviour but to which they do not actually belong.

One traditional membership group used is socioeconomic groups. The table below shows the UK socioeconomic groupings which are still regularly quoted:

Group Title	Social Status	Occupation
A	Upper	Higher Management/ Professional
B	Middle	Middle Management / Admin/ Professional
C1	Lower Middle	Supervisory/ Junior Management
C2	Skilled Working	Artisans /Crafts
D	Unskilled Working	Manual Unskilled
E	On Benefit	Pensioners/ Casual Workers/ Unemployed

Table 8.1 Socioeconomic groups (based on NRS Social Grades)

The rationale is that differences in socio economic class imply differences in disposable income, education and attitudes.

However, this is constantly being challenged. Social class is not as rigid as it used to be – people are more upwardly mobile and the barriers are breaking down. In addition socio-economic groups are determined by the head of the household. Due to significant changes in working patterns and family structures over recent years this approach is open to question as other members of the family group may behave very differently from the family 'head'.

In addition people do not just belong to one group. Individuals usually belong to a 'primary' and 'secondary membership group' - of which socioeconomic class may be one.

In addition, there are also:

- **Family groups -** despite changes over the years in the shape of the family unit, the family is still a strong influence on purchasing behaviour.
- **Aspirational groups -** these are groups to which an individual would like to belong such as professional bodies or 'gangs' - some may be more realistic than others.
- **Dissociative groups** - these are groups to which an individual does not want to belong or does not want to be seen to belong.

By identifying the membership and reference groups customers belong to or might aspire to marketing messages can be tailored to appeal to the values they are most likely to hold.

8.6 Culture

Simplistically, corporate culture has been described by Deal and Kennedy as: "the way things get done around here" (Deal and Kennedy, 1982). In other words, culture is the result of interactions with the world around us; our environment shapes us as individuals. It is the result of a learning process and comprises a broad set of values, perceptions, preferences and behaviour patterns.

A culture will also have sub-cultures such as religious, ethnic groups and geographical areas which are all likely to have their own specific characteristics. In an organisation sub-cultures may exist in different departments or social groupings.

It is important that marketers understand culture for a number of reasons. Culture is a powerful determinant of how people behave, their needs and values. In addition different cultures in different countries or markets will have different values, beliefs and attitudes. These can be powerful influences in terms of taboos and requirements.

8.7 Behavioural economics

The concept of behavioural economics has been around since the late 1970s but came to the fore with the publication of 'Nudge' by Thaler and Sunstein (Thaler and Sunstein, 2008). Initially it was used primarily to analyse financial decision making but since then it has been applied to marketing and notably to governmental social marketing.

There are seven relevant principles of behavioural economics and they all have relevance to marketing and purchasing behaviour:

- **Loss aversion** - the principle here is that people will work harder to avoid losing something than they will to get it in the first place. They ascribe a disproportionately higher value to an item that they already own, in comparison to one they are being offered, despite what they may have originally paid for it. Behavioural economics tells us that it can be twice as painful to lose an item as it was enjoyable to acquire it in the first place.
- **The power of NOW** - consumers engage less with future events than they do with current events.
- **Scarcity value** - when we perceive something to be scarce it has a greater value in our eyes. Conversely, when we perceive it to be plentiful its perceived value falls.
- **Goal dilution** - it is harder to achieve multiple goals than goals pursued individually.
- **Chunking** - parts are easier than wholes. The way a task is presented affects people's willingness to take it on and complete it.
- **Price perception** - people use price as an indicator of quality and value.
- **Choice architecture** - an individual's choice is relative to what they can have not necessarily exactly what they want. People choose based on what is available or what they are aware is available.

All of these have implications for marketing communications.

For example, keep things simple, get the timing right, balance value and price, make sure your product or service is available and that your market knows about it.

Another key factor that should be taken into account is **risk**. With every buying decision comes risk; higher value, less frequent purchases have more risk; and everyone has a different propensity towards risk. By identifying the dominant forms of risk present at any time, it is then possible to design messages that can reduce perceived risk. The list below identifies some of the different forms of risk:

- **Performance risk –** will the product perform as expected?
- **Financial risk –** is the product or service affordable?
- **Physical risk –** will the product actually harm the consumer?
- **Social risk –** what will others think about the purchase?
- **Ego risk –**am I doing the right thing?
- **Time risk –** how much time and effort needs to be spent making the purchase. This can be a significant risk factor. For example, anxiety covered by long delays, queries, etc.

You may not be able to factor in all of the 'individual' and other influences on your buyers' behaviour that we have looked at but being aware of them and considering which might have the most relevance for your market and brand will help you make your communications that much more effective.

8.8 Learning

Why does learning matter? Because how, when and what we learn influences our behaviour. Honey and Mumford state that there are four learning styles (Honey and Mumford, 1982):

- **Activist –** learns best from active involvement in the task, such as participating in business games and team competitions. An activist is hands on and will get thoroughly involved in experiences.
- **Pragmatist –** learns best when there is a link between new information and real life, such as case studies and role play.

The pragmatist will tend to only find out about something if there is a direct link to a practical problem. Generally, this type of learner will not spend long periods of time reading around products and services that are of little interest to them at a given point in time.

- **Reflector** – learns best by reviewing what has happened. They like to observe the world around them, to think about what they have observed and then choose how to act.
- **Theorist** – learns well when new information can be linked to theoretical contexts, absorbing new ideas when they are distanced from real life. The theorist seeks to understand underlying concepts or ideas first before applying them.

David Kolb also developed a model of learning styles. This sets out four learning styles based on a four stage 'learning cycle' illustrated in Figure 8.2.

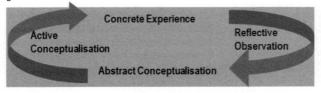

Figure 8.2 Kolb's learning cycle (Kolb *et. al.*, 1995)
KOLB, DAVID A.; OSLAND, JOYCE S.; RUBIN, IRWIN M., ORGANIZATIONAL BEHAVIOR: AN EXPERIENTIAL APPROACH, 6th,©1995. Printed and Electronically reproduced by permission of Pearson Education, Inc., Upper Saddle River, New Jersey.

In the cycle of learning the 'concrete experience' provides a basis for 'reflective observation' which in turn enables 'abstract concepts' to be developed which are then actively experimented with in turn generating new experiences. Kolb argues that ideally a learner goes through all four stages of the cycle (though not always): experiencing, reflecting, thinking and acting. This may appear simplistic but if you think about the way in which you learn it should strike a chord with your own experiences.

Memory is clearly an important factor in learning. The following definitions were sourced from human-memory.net (Mastin, 2010):

Sensory memory

Sensory memory is the shortest-term element of memory. It is the ability to retain impressions of sensory information after the original stimuli have ended. It acts as a kind of buffer for stimuli received through the five senses of **sight, hearing, smell, taste and touch,** which are retained accurately, but very briefly. For example, the ability to look at something and remember what it looked like with just a second of observation is an example of sensory memory.

Short-term memory

Short-term memory acts as a kind of "scratch-pad" for temporary recall of the information which is being processed at any point in time, and has been referred to as "the brain's Post-It note". It can be thought of as the ability to remember and process information at the same time. It holds a small amount of information (typically around 7 items or even less) in mind in an active, readily-available state for a short period of time (typically from 10 to 15 seconds, or sometimes up to a minute).

(Short term memory is thought to fade at 34–35 years old. This affects the way that people learn).

Long-term memory

Long-term memory is, obviously enough, intended for storage of information over a long period of time. Despite our everyday impressions of forgetting, it seems likely that long-term memory actually decays very little over time, and can store a seemingly unlimited amount of information almost indefinitely. Indeed, there is some debate as to whether we actually ever "forget" anything at all, or whether it just becomes increasingly difficult to access or retrieve certain items from memory.

Short-term memories can become long-term memory through the process of consolidation, involving rehearsal and meaningful association.

Unlike short-term memory (which relies mostly on an acoustic, and to a lesser extent on a visual code for storing information), long-term memory encodes information for storage semantically i.e. based on meaning and association. However, there is also some evidence that long-term memory does also encode to some extent by sound. For example, when we cannot quite remember a word but it is "on the tip of my tongue", this is usually based on the sound of a word, not its meaning.

With marketing communications clearly recall is very important. So what are the factors that influence retrieval of information?

- **Mood congruence** – the 'mood congruent memory effect' is that people are more likely to remember communications that are in tune with their mood i.e. happy people will recollect advertising that was happy whereas sad people will remember sad messages more than happy ones (Mayer et al,1995).
- **Familiarity** – by associating new material with something that is already familiar, the chances of it being remembered are greatly improved. This is of particular importance when we consider brand recognition and product recall.
- **Salience** – something that is especially relevant is more likely to be recalled. This may be relevance to a learning style. So timing, targeting and relevance are important.
- **Pictorial vs. verbal cues** – recognition appears to come more readily than recall. For example, it is easier to recognise a face than to recall a name. It is important to provide appropriate cues that bring brand recognition and aid product recall.
- **Drives** – a force urging action.
- **Stimuli** – trigger the drives.
- **Responses** – by the consumer to the product.
- **Reinforcement** – this is a key aspect of marketing today in both relationship and experiential marketing.

There are a number of lessons in all of this:

- If we can understand how our target audiences learn and take in information, we can ascertain which communications techniques will motivate our customers.
- Understanding that people learn in different ways means we can develop communications that are tailored to how they like to find out about things: by thinking, by doing, by feeling and by watching.
- As we grow older our attitudes and learning styles become more rigid with age. This has relevance for communications to the 'grey market'.
- Understanding how memory works enables communications to turn sensory memory into short term memory into long term memory.
- Recall and recognition respond best to different triggers: sound and vision.
- Understanding how people retrieve information highlights the importance of mood congruence, relevance, familiarity, pictorial or verbal cues, stimuli and reinforcement.

Chapter 9: Communication and Learning Models

Now that we have looked at some of the key influences on buyer behaviour and at how people learn we also need to look at the process of communication and the influence this has on our target audience. We have already looked at Fill's DRIP model in Chapter 1 which recognises that communications can differentiate, reinforce, inform and persuade. There are a number of additional models which examine the process of communication and the effects it has on learning, attitudes and behaviour.

9.1 Shannon's 'general' model

Shannon's 'general' model (see Figure 9.1) was the first general model of the communication process (Shannon,1948). It breaks down the communications process to explain how communication happens and why communication sometimes fails.

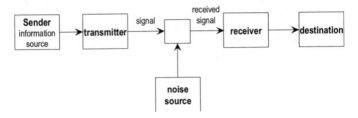

Figure 9.1 Shannon's 'General' model (Shannon, 1948)

The model has eight elements

1. **The information source** - the creator of the message, the marketer or marketing department.
2. **The message** - which is created by the information source and could be the features of the product.
3. **A transmitter** - essentially how the communication is broadcast e.g. TV, Radio, Website, etc.

4. **The signal** - the transmitter has now encapsulated or converted the message into a signal to be sent over a channel. Given the limitations of the channels chosen the signal may need to amend or alter the message e.g. radio cannot show images.

5. **A carrier or channel** - is in essence the media by which the advert is conveyed.

6. **Noise** - this is the background activity that disrupts the smooth reception of a marketing message. The noise might come from competing adverts or alternative products which may distract the consumer. Some media will have greater noise than others.

7. **A receiver** - in Shannon's original idea this was the receiving telephone handset. In reality this is the device used to receive the message by the prospect or customer. In face-to-face communication this would be a set of ears (sound) and eyes (gesture). Or today it could be a PC or mobile phone which highlights the problem of consumers seeing something different from what was sent. For example consider users of a smartphone or other mobile device where the rendition of an email or webpage may vary significantly depending on the make of the device.

8. **A destination** - the person (a prospect or customer) who reads or sees the message.

Shannon's model is a useful simplification of the communications process and gives some real insights into the issues of promotion. However it presents the communications as a one way 'push' and therefore really needs to be amended with a feedback loop. In addition it assumes that, despite the Noise, the message does get through. This is addressed in the Intermediary Model of Communication.

9.2 The intermediary model

This is often referred to as a gatekeeper model and was developed by Katz from 'The Two-Step Flow of Communication: An Up-Do-Date Report on an Hypothesis', *Public Opinion Quarterly* by permission of Oxford University Press:

| Speaker | ⟶ | Gatekeeper | ⟶ | Audience |

Figure 9.2 Intermediary model (Katz, 1957)

Intermediaries or 'gatekeepers' have the ability to change messages or to prevent them from reaching an audience. Examples in mass media are editors who choose some content in preference to others or based on editorial policy; moderators of internet discussion forums; or filters on emails.

There are many intermediary roles: they have the ability to decide what messages are seen, the context in which they are seen, and when they are seen. They could be seen as active 'noise' in the context of the General Model.

9.3 The transactional model

One of the issues with both of the models discussed above is that they do not take into account the importance of two-way communication which is important as feedback can change the message being communicated. And do not forget that feedback is likely to experience noise as the initial communication did.

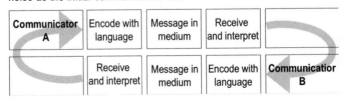

Figure 9.3 The transactional model

This model is very interpersonal and assumes an equality between the communicators. Whilst this is rarely the case in the offline world it can apply (strongly) to the online world where anyone can join in a social media discussion or forum, be heard by thousands and affect the impact of communications.

9.4 The ecological model
The ecological model of communication was developed by Davis Foulger to address some of the shortcomings of the earlier models (Foulger, 2004).

In this model, reception of any advert or communication is not automatic; people have the ability to consciously and unconsciously screen out messages; it is recognised that some media are more appealing than others dependent upon audience; and finally that when interpreting messages the use of language (verbal and non-verbal) is important. Thus, the choice of message, media and language affect the effectiveness of a communication.

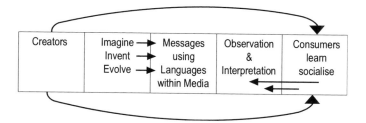

Figure 9.4 Ecological model

9.5 Learning hierarchy models
Having looked at models of the communication process there are also a number of models which look at how communications affect learning, attitudes and behaviour. Initially the view taken was that communication affects information, then attitudes and then behaviour. This is known as the Learning Hierarchy. However, not all theorists agreed.

Ray et al concluded that there were 3 basic models depending on the communication context (Ray et al, 1973):

Learning Hierarchy:	**Learn, Feel, Do**
The Dissonance-Attribution Hierarchy:	**Do, Feel, Learn**
The Low-Involvement Hierarchy:	**Learn, Do, Feel**

Learn, feel and do are also known as:

'Learn'	'Feel'	'Do'
Thinking	Feeling/attitudes	Behaviour
Cognitive	Affective	Conative

Gagne proposed a system of classifying different types of learning based on the complexity of the mental processes involved. He identified eight basic types of learning, and arranged these in a hierarchical order (Gagne, 1965). According to Gagne, the higher orders of learning are built upon the lower levels, requiring progressively greater amounts of previous learning for their success. The lowest four orders tend to focus on the more responsive and behavioural aspects of learning, while the highest four focus on the more cognitive aspects:

- **Signal learning** – this is the simplest form of learning, and consists essentially of subjecting the consumer to a stimulus which produces a desired response naturally after a certain number of repetitions. The application of classical conditioning in facilitating human learning is, however, very limited.
- **Stimulus-response learning** – is similar to the above but with an added reinforcement schedule based on the use of 'rewards' presented after the response. It is this type of conditioning that forms the basis of programmed learning.
- **Chaining** – this is when the learner develops the ability to connect two or more previously-learned stimulus-response bonds into a linked sequence. It is the process whereby marketers would be able to build loyalty through continued rewards.

- **Verbal association** — this is a form of chaining in which the links between the items being connected are verbal in nature. Verbal association is one of the key processes in the development of language skills.
- **Discrimination learning** — this involves developing the ability to make appropriate, and different, responses to a series of similar messages that differ in a systematic way. The process is made more complex by 'noise' or 'interference', where one piece of learning inhibits another. Interference is thought to be one of the main causes of forgetting. Of course, in marketing interference can occur from competitor advertising.
- **Concept learning** — this involves developing the ability to make a consistent response to different stimuli that form a common class or category of some sort. It forms the basis of the ability to generalise, classify, etc.
- **Rule learning** — this is a very-high-level cognitive process that involves being able to learn relationships between concepts and apply these relationships in different situations, including situations not previously encountered. It forms the basis of the learning of general rules, procedures, etc.
- **Problem solving** — this is the highest level of cognitive process. It involves developing the ability to invent a complex rule, algorithm or procedure for the purpose of solving one particular problem, and then using the method to solve other problems of a similar nature.

Gagne's learning hierarchy demonstrates that it is important for us to understand that people have different abilities to take in information, and different learning styles. This is why it is so vital to understand our markets and consumers and tailor and build our communication. Our audience proceeds from learning about an idea or innovation, to developing favourable attitudes, to adaptation of behaviour. Each step is assumed to be a precondition for the next (hence the idea of a hierarchy of effects). In this instance: **Learn, Feel, Do**.

Dissonance-attribution hierarchy

The Dissonance-Attribution Hierarchy adopts the reverse sequence. Ray et al believed that a new behaviour experience, such as trying a new product or exposure to a marketing message, leads to a change in attitudes/beliefs which in turn leads to learning about the new product in order to support the behaviour (Ray et al, op.cit.).

Products involved in this hierarchy tend to be high value, high risk such as home entertainment products and luxury goods. Having made such a purchase consumers actively seek information that supports the purchase that they have made. As a result, much of the promotion in these categories centres on post- purchase reassurance in order to reduce consumer dissonance. In this instance the hierarchy is: **Do, Feel, Learn.**

Low-involvement hierarchy

The 'low-involvement' hierarchy developed by Krugman relates to a situation in which there is little differentiation in the communication message and as a result, the receivers have a low level of interest and attention (Krugman, 1965). According to Ray, this is typical of watching advertising on the television, where attention is casual (Ray, op. cit.).

He suggests that products such as packaged goods and convenience items are most commonly influenced by the low-involvement hierarchy. In this instance it is repetition of the message that builds familiarity or learning, eventually prompting the customer to try the new product and then change their attitudes/views based on the experience. The sequence is: **Learn, Do, Feel**.

9.6 Response hierarchy models

In addition to the learning hierarchy models there are a number of models which look at consumers' response to communications. The simplest and probably best known model is AIDA.

AIDA

The AIDA model was developed by Edward Strong (Strong, 1925). AIDA stands for:

- **Attention** – Awareness of a brand, product or service
- **Interest** – Taking an interest in that brand
- **Desire** – Engaging a willingness to purchase from that brand
- **Action** – Purchasing a product or service from that brand

The model is simple, which may explain its lasting appeal, and was developed in an attempt to explain how personal selling is conducted. The stages are shown in a linear fashion and the assumption is that action will take place naturally as a result of moving through the first three steps. The model helps in understanding the 'hierarchy of effects' theory. However, in today's marketplace, the model is often seen as overly simplistic and a number of variants have been developed from the original AIDA model (see Table 9.1).

Adoption	Hierarchy of Effects	DAGMAR
Awareness	Awareness	Unawareness
Interest	Knowledge	Awareness
Evaluation	Liking Preference	Comprehension
Trial	Conviction	Conviction
Adoption	Purchase	Action

Table 9.1 Response hierarchy models

Diffusion of Innovation or 'Adoption' Model

As you can see from Table 9.1, this model looks very similar to the AIDA model. The main difference is that 'Evaluation' has been added between 'Interest' and 'Trial'. The other elements may be different in name but are identical to the structure of the AIDA model. However, this model was in fact developed by Strong to look at adoption of innovation by consumers and sought to explain how new innovations spread through society – with some consumers being innovators and early adopters, followed by the early and late majority, with the laggards following in the rear (Rogers, 1962).

DAGMAR Model

Defining Advertising Goals for Measured Advertising Results (DAGMAR) was developed by Russell Colley (Colley, 1995). As the name suggests, Colley developed the model for setting advertising objectives and measuring their achievement. He wanted to show marketers that they could measure the return on their advertising spend by setting clear objectives and distinguishing advertising objectives (such as brand awareness) form marketing and corporate objectives (such as sales).

He identified five stages that a consumer goes through towards purchase: unawareness, awareness, comprehension, conviction, and action. Again similarities with AIDA and the Adoption model can be seen but this time 'unawareness' has been added as an initial stage.

Hierarchy of Effects Model

The Hierarchy of Effects model developed by Lavidge and Steiner suggests that there are six steps from seeing an advertisement to purchase (Learnmarketing, 2013).

- **Awareness** – the customer is exposed to advertisements (and other marketing communications) and becomes aware of the product. This is a critical and difficult step because there is no guarantee a customer will notice the advert or remember the product afterwards.

- **Knowledge** – the customer is now aware of the product and wants to find out more. At this stage it is important to ensure product information is readily available in-store or on the web.
- **Liking** – based on information collected the customer develops a liking for the product - at this stage promoting the right product qualities and attributes is essential.
- **Preference** – by this stage, consumers may still have a number of alternative brands that they like. Consequently highlighting a brand's USP or distinctive benefits is key.
- **Conviction** – by now the customer has developed a preference for a brand and the task is to convince them to purchase. This could be achieved by providing a free trial or by providing reassurance and reducing any risk/doubts in their minds.
- **Purchase** – the customer is now ready to purchase but it is still not a done deal! If the customer is frustrated or disappointed at any touch points they may walk away. It is important to ensure satisfaction at these touch points such as ensuring a simple ordering process. Many websites fail at this point.

A final point to note is that this model is referred to as a hierarchy not just because a customer has to advance through the steps in sequence but because the number of customers who progress to each stage will decline. Not everyone who becomes aware of a product will want to find out more about it; not everyone who finds out more will like what they find out.

There are many other models of the communication process, learning and buyer behaviour – some very complex, some specific to digital communications or particular markets. However, the models we have covered here should give you a good insight into the issues and possibilities to help you make your marketing communications more effective.

References

Baker (2012) *Marketing Week*, [online], http://www.marketingweek.co.uk/news/lynx-debuts-first-sound-activated-cinema-ad/4002840.article, (Accessed 1 August 2013)

Brassington, F and Petit, S (2007) *Principles of Marketing*, Financial Times/Prentice Hall

BSI Group (2013), *ISO 10002 Customer Satisfaction, Complaints*, [online] http://www.bsigroup.hk/Assessment-and-certification-services/Management-systems/Standards-and-schemes/ISO-10002/ (Accessed 4 September 2013)

CIPR 2011, *What is PR?*, [Online], http://www.cipr.co.uk/content/careers-cpd/careers-pr/what-pr, (Accessed 1 August 2013)

Christopher M., Payne A., and Ballantyne D. (2002) Relationship Marketing: Creating Stakeholder Value, 2nd edition, Butterworth-Heinemann (ISBN-10: 0750648392 ISBN-13: 978-0750648394)

Colley R. (1995) Dagmar, Defining Advertising Goals for Measured Advertising Results, NTC Business Books 1995

Customer Loyalty Institute (2011) *What is Customer Loyalty?*, [online], http://www.customerloyalty.org/what-is-customer-loyalty/, (Accessed 11 August 2013)

Deal T. and Kennedy A. (1982) *Corporate Cultures: The Rites and Rituals of Corporate Life, Penguin Books*

Fill C. (2011) *Essentials of Marketing Communications*, Prentice Hall

Fill C. (2006) *Simply Marketing Communications*, Financial Times/ Prentice Hall

Foulger D 2004 *An Ecological Model of the Communication Process*, [online], http://davis.foulger.info/papers/ecologicalModelOfCommunication.htm, (Accessed 9 August 2013)

Gagne R M (1965) *Conditions of Learning*, Holt, Rinehart and Winston

Giddens N. and Hofmann A. (2011) Building Your Brand with Brand Line Extensions, online, available from: http://www.extension.iastate.edu/agdm/wholefarm/html/c5-52.html, (Accessed 7 July 2013)

Goldfingle G. and Lawson A. (2013) Asda profits increase despite flat like-for-likes over Christmas as it plots George's online expansion, *Retail Week*, online, http://www.retail-week.com/companies/asda/asda-profits-increase-despite-flat-christmas-like-for-likes/5046492.article

Grunig J.E and Hunt T. (1984, *Managing Public Relations*, Holt, Rinehart & Winston

Gummesson E. (2002) The New Marketing – Developing Long Term Interactive Relationships, *Long Range Planning*, Vol. 20/4, No.10

Hallberg G. (2004) Is your loyalty programme really building loyalty? Why increasing emotional attachment, not just repeat buying, is key to maximising programme success, *Journal of Targeting, Measurement and Analysis for Marketing*, 12, p 231–241

Honey P. and Mumford A. (1982) Manual of Learning Styles, Peter Honey Publications

Jobber D. (2007) *Principles and Practice of Marketing* (5th edition), McGraw-Hill Education

Katz, E. (1957) The Two-Step Flow of Communication: An Up-Do-Date Report on an Hypothesis, *Public Opinion Quarterly*, 21

Kolb, D.A., Osland, J.S., Rubin, I.M (1995) Organizational behavior: An experiential approach, Pearson Education, Inc.

Kotler, P (1991) Principles of Marketing, Prentice Hall

Krugman H. E. (1965), *The Impact of Television Advertising: Learning Without Involvement*, Public Opinion Quarterly 29, no. 3 (Fall), p 349-56

Learnmarketing (2013) Hierarchy of Effects Model, [online] http://www.learnmarketing.net/hierarchy_of_effects_model.html (Accessed 10 Oct 2013)

Maslow, A. H. (1943) A theory of human motivation, *Psychological Review*, Vol 50(4), Jul 1943, pp.370-396.

Mastin L. (2010) Human-memory.net, online, http://www.human-memory.net/types_sensory.html, (Accessed 12 August 2013)

Mayer J.D., McCormick L.J. and Strong S.E. (1995) Mood-Congruent Memory and Natural Mood: New Evidence, *Personality and Social Psychology Bulletin*, 21, 736-746

Mendelow A. (1991) *Stakeholder Mapping*, Proceedings of the 2nd International Conference on Information Systems, Cambridge, MA

Porter M.E. (1980) *Competitive Strategy*, Free Press

Ray M.L. , Sawyer A. G., Rothschild M. L., Heeler R. M., Strong E. C. and Reed, J. B. (1973) Marketing Communications and the Hierarchy of Effects, *New Models for Mass Communication Research*, ed. Peter Clarke, Sage Publishing, p 147-76

Riezebos R. (2002) *Brand Management: A Theoretical and Practical Approach*, Financial Times/ Prentice Hall

Rogers E. M. (1962) *Diffusion of innovations*,Free Press

Shannon C. (1948) A Mathematical Theory of Communication, *Bell System Technical Journal* 27 (July and October) p 379–423, p 623–656

Smith P.R. (2004) *Marketing Communications* (4th edition), Kogan Page

SOSTAC® is a registered trade mark of PR Smith, author of The SOSTAC® Guide to Writing the Perfect Plan (eBook) available from www.prsmith.org and www.facebook.com/prsmithmarketing and Amazon.

Strong E.K. (1925) The Psychology of Selling and Advertising, McGraw-Hill

Thaler R.H. and Sunstein C.R. (2008) *Nudge: Improving Decisions About Health, Wealth and Happiness*, Penguin

VanAuken B 2011 *Exploring the Role of Brand Equity In Brand Extension*, The Blake Project, online, http://www.brandingstrategyinsider.com/brand_extension/, (Accessed 11 August 2013)

Vaughn R. (1980) How advertising works: A planning model, *Journal of Advertising Research*, Volume 20 Advertising Research Foundation

Ward B. (2013) The Voice of the Customer Meets the Voice of the Expert, http://www.affinitymc.com/voice-customer-meets-voice-expert/ (Accessed 10 Oct 2013)

Wilson A. (2006) *Marketing Research: An Integrated Approach*, Pearson Education UK

Index

Cambridge Marketing Handbooks

This Communications Handbook is one in a series of Handbooks for marketing practitioners and students, designed to cover the full spectrum of the Marketing Mix. The other Handbooks include:

- Products
- Pricing Points
- Services
- Philosophy
- Research
- Stakeholder
- Law
- Digital
- Distribution